SOVEREIGNTY AND SALVATION IN THE VERNACULAR, 1050–1150

MEDIEVAL GERMAN TEXTS IN BILINGUAL EDITIONS, 1

SOVEREIGNTY AND SALVATION IN THE VERNACULAR, 1050–1150

DAS EZZOLIED
DAS ANNOLIED
DIE KAISERCHRONIK, VV. 247–667
DAS LOB SALOMONS
HISTORIA JUDITH

**Introduction, Translations, and Notes
by James A. Schultz**

Published for TEAMS
(The Consortium for the Teaching of the Middle Ages)

by

Medieval Institute Publications
Western Michigan University
Kalamazoo, Michigan — 2000

Library of Congress Cataloging-in-Publication Data

Sovereignty and salvation in the vernacular, 1050-1150 / introduction, translations, and notes by James A. Schultz.
    p.cm. -- (Medieval German texts in bilingual editions ; 1)
    Introd. in English, texts in English and Middle High German.
    Includes bibliographical references and index.
    Contents: Das Ezzolied -- Das Annolied -- Die Kaiserchronik, vv. 247-667 -- Das Lob Salomons -- Historia Judith.
    ISBN 1-58044-062-2 (alk. paper)
    1. German poetry--Middle High German, 1050-1500--Translations into English. I. Schultz, James A. (James Alfred), 1947-II. Series.

PT1396 .S68 2000
831'.0320801--dc21   00-020965

ISBN 1-58044-062-2

Cover Design by Linda K. Judy

Printed in the United States of America

CONTENTS

ACKNOWLEDGEMENTS

The text of the *Annolied* is taken from *Das Annolied: Mittelhochdeutsch und Neuhochdeutsch*, ed., trans., commentary by Eberhard Nellmann, Stuttgart 1979 (Universal-Bibliothek,1416), by permission of Philipp Reclam jun.Verlag.

The texts of the *Ezzolied*, the *Lob Salomons* and the *Historia Judith* are taken from *Kleinere deutsche Gedichte des 11. und 12. Jahrhunderts*, ed. Werner Schröder, vol. 1, Tübingen 1972 (Altdeutsche Textbibliothek, 71), by permission of Max Niemeyer Verlag.

FOREWORD

The Medieval German Texts series is designed for classroom use in
German and Medieval Studies as well as for the more advanced scholar in
fields adjacent to that of German literature: the historian, latinist, theolo-
gian or romanist who wishes to extend her reading and research across
those largely artificial borders that still divide medievalists unnecessarily.
To this end we want to make available, in modern English translation as
well as in the original, texts from the mid-eleventh to the end of the
fifteenth centuries which are not yet part of the general study and
discussion of vernacular European literature and which at the same time
are particularly likely to contribute new and special perspectives to that
discussion once they have become more generally known and available.

True, there is no shortage of modern English translations of medieval
German texts, from "pre-courtly" epic verse narrative to thirteenth-century
lyric poetry and from minor Arthurian romance to late medieval mystic
prose or satire in verse. Some of these translations, particularly those of
"classics" like Wolfram von Eschenbach's *Parzival* and *Willehalm*,
Gottfried von Strassburg's *Tristan,* or the *Nibelungenlied*, are very good
indeed and have served their purpose well; others are not so good, long out
of print or otherwise not readily available. But anyone taking the trouble
to assemble and peruse this small virtual library would get at least a
superficial impression of how some of the main genres of Western
medieval literature in the vernacular are represented in this particular
vernacular, Middle High German.[1]

At the same time, the positive aspects of this state of affairs only partly
disguise two general deficits that become apparent once we ask ourselves
to what extent our hypothetical reader has been enabled to understand and

---

[1] The term is here used loosely to cover the four and one-half centuries indicated
above, without the customary and always debatable subdivisions, including "early
modern" toward the end. For a concise survey of major trends and changes in this
mega-period see my article, "Middle High German Literature," listed below in the
bibliography to this volume. Treatment of individual authors and (anonymous) texts in
the *Dictionary of the Middle Ages* is very uneven, and inquiring minds will fare much
better with the *Verfasserlexikon*, cited in the same bibliography.

appreciate what, apart from their language, may be specifically German about texts written in German during that period. First of all, choices have been guided on the whole by a concept that privileges "major" works and the "belles lettres," whatever that may mean in medieval terms, or to put it differently, selections have concentrated on the kinds of texts that constitute German examples of what could be called the international canon of "high-culture" genres and themes. It seems therefore that the time has come to draw attention to forms of writing and literary expression which may serve better to highlight some of the differences that character-ize the process in which German evolves in its own particular way as the writing class's vehicle of literary and cultural expression within the shifting borders and under diverse political, social or cultural conditions in various parts of the Empire.

The second major deficit, from this point of view, is the exclusion of the Middle High German original from most of these publications. Such decisions depend on the intended audience, of course. Translations that represent the text on their own have their place in this area of linguistic mediation between cultures just as they do in any other. When, however, the primary target is a predominantly academic audience, it ought to be given the incentive as well as the opportunity to consult the original along with the translation. By the same token, the primary purpose of such translations becomes to facilitate such access, allowing readers to engage the original German according to their own special needs and at their own pace.

In line with general TEAMS policy, the price of the volumes in this new series will be kept low with an eye particularly to the student. In terms of content, they should appeal to student and scholar alike through their focus on what is, from a Pan-European point of view, "different" in a variety of possible ways, exemplifying something not easily found in other vernacular literatures of the same period. That may be an unusual generic configura-tion; a special perspective on an international theme or a particularly interesting response to the common Latin tradition; a form of transmission or intertextuality not known from elsewhere at that time but of general significance for the development of vernacular writing; and, not least, a special kind of author or intended audience.

For the early period, such differences are self-evident as a matter of comparative chronology. Not long after the first flowering of vernacular writing had come to a halt in Anglo-Saxon England and in the largely isolated monastic communities that created or recorded texts in what is known as Old High German, the southern and western regions of the German-speaking area entered a second period of substantial and, in terms of the vernaculars, remarkably original composition of religious verse and prose, mostly monastic in origin but often with strong overtones of political, even dynastic, and social engagement and hardly comparable at all to the early literary production in French, Anglo-Norman, Provençal or (slightly later) Old Norse. That is the reason why the first two volumes of the series are designed to showcase some of this literature from the period from roughly 1050 to 1150. Professor Schultz's introduction to this, the first, volume describes some of the phenomena that are characteristic not only of the texts he has selected and of their contexts but of this whole phase of vernacular writing at various ecclesiastic centers. The second volume, with a translation and introduction by James A. Rushing, Jr., will be devoted exclusively to the biblical poetry of the *inclusa*, Frau Ava, who died in 1127 and who is the first woman, as far as we know, to have put her name to a substantial body of vernacular verse during the western Middle Ages.

Further volumes in this series will not follow any particular chronological order. Obviously, much depends on the availability of expert translators, and the editorial board welcomes suggestions and proposals.[2] These bilingual editions will present, on facing pages, the text of the original in the standard critical edition minus its scholarly apparatus, and a translation in straightforward English prose which reproduces meaning as faithfully as possible, compatible with modern idiomatic usage. A brief introduction, accompanied by an equally brief bibliography, will situate the text in its historical environment, including particularly its transmission. Explanatory notes will be kept to a minimum, confined primarily to essential background information; special features of the manuscript evidence such as pictures; corrupt text passages or especially difficult translator's decisions. Since pictures are an integral part of the representation of the text wherever

---

[2] High on our own list of *desiderata* is Thomasin von Zerclaere's didactic verse tract, *Der welsche Gast*, which Thomasin, a trilingual Friulian, composed in 1215/16 and addressed to the German-speaking lay nobility, the "literary public" to the northwest. It is, among other things, the oldest extant vernacular text whose author included a complementary program of illustrations to enhance the effectiveness of his overall message.

they occur,[3] *Medieval German Texts* will reproduce this pictorial compo-
nent of the manuscript tradition in one form or another. In some cases, such
as Frau Ava, reproductions can be included in the volume itself. Richer and
more diverse traditions, like that of Thomasin's work, may be stored on the
TEAMS web site.

With this series we offer students and scholars of the Western Middle
Ages access to German vernacular texts and textual traditions that should
be known more widely. Partly for their own sake, but particularly also
because they shed significant light on the process of vernacularization that
took place everywhere and promise to help foster the kind of cooperation
among disciplines that is at the heart of the medievalist enterprise.

PRINCETON, DECEMBER 1999   MICHAEL CURSCHMANN

---

[3] This material has been compiled and catalogued systematically since the early 1960s
by the Kommission für Deutsche Literatur des Mittelalters at the Bavarian Academy of
Sciences in Munich, and the first volumes have appeared in this decade: Hella
Frühmorgen-Voss and Norbert H. Ott, *Katalog der deutschsprachigen illustrierten
Handschriften des Mittelalters*, 3 vols. to date (Munich: C. H. Beck, 1991; 1996; 1999
[vol.3, 1–3]).

INTRODUCTION

Writing in German began about 750 in the language we now call Old High German. The missionary work of the Carolingian Church provided the initial impetus for this innovation, and the efforts of Ludwig the German to consolidate his rule in the eastern empire inspired the production of texts a century later. Shortly after 900, however, reasons to write in German seem to have lost their force, and, except for a few isolated efforts, such writing ceases. When it resumes, shortly after 1050, the language has changed considerably, into what is known as Middle High German (MHG), and the cultural context that supported writing in the vernacular has changed as well. The texts in this volume are among the first to have been written in this new context. Although they are the first, they are nevertheless texts of great power, and include two, the *Ezzolied* and the *Annolied*, that would be on anyone's list of the monuments of medieval German literature.

But these are not the principal reasons for offering them in English translation. We do so rather in the belief that they will be of interest to medievalists who might not have access to them in the original. We believe they will be of interest because they represent a kind of writing — at the intersection of ecclesiastical and secular power, drawing on the whole range of medieval Latin learning, yet written in vernacular verse — that is not found elsewhere in the European Middle Ages. In addition, they may be of use in teaching since, although relatively short, they illustrate a great number of characteristic medieval ways of writing and can be directly linked to a number of quite remarkable historical figures.

Because it offers the easiest way of introducing the individual texts, I will begin by describing their production and transmission. To an extraordinary extent, these texts were subject to expansion, revision, appropriation, and other forms of what has been called "productive reception." I will turn then to questions of intellectual tradition and poetics. These texts find remarkably effective means of expressing the Latin learning of their age in a MHG vernacular that was just beginning its career as a medium for written poetry. Finally I will try to describe something of the cultural context that enabled this new synthesis. With bracing directness these texts represent the concentration of political, ecclesiastical, and cultural power in the centers where they were produced.

PRODUCTION AND PRODUCTIVE RECEPTION

Although the *Ezzolied* is probably the oldest text in Middle High German, we are surprisingly well informed about the circumstances of its composition. One source of this information is the first strophe of the later, expanded version of the text, which tells us that Gunther, bishop of Bamberg, commissioned one of his clerics, Ezzo, to write the text of a song and that Wille composed the tune. Ezzo's song must have been written, then, during the years of Gunther's episcopate, 1057–65. A second source, the *Vita Altmanni*, the Latin life of another bishop, reports that a "canon and scholar" named Ezzo "composed a song about the miracles of Christ in his native tongue" on a pilgrimage that Bishop Gunther led to the Holy Land in 1064–65 — although scholars have wondered if the song might have been composed earlier and only sung on the pilgrimage. This double record, in German and in Latin, provides us with more detailed information about the composition of the *Ezzolied* than we have for almost any other MHG text, including the most famous. It suggests that contemporaries recognized the *Ezzolied* for the pathbreaking accomplishment that it was: the first poetic text of the high Middle Ages to join Latin learning and the German vernacular.

The *Ezzolied* survives in two versions. The earlier version is fragmentary, breaking off just before the end of the seventh strophe. It is known to scholars as the Straßburg *Ezzolied* after the location of the single manuscript in which it is found. It celebrates the glory of God in the Creation, remembers the Fall and the night of sin that followed. The later version, assumed to have been written 1120–30, is known as the Vorau *Ezzolied* since it is found in a manuscript in Vorau (in Styria, Austria). Unlike the earlier version, the later one is complete. It is also expanded. The last, seventh strophe of the earlier version corresponds to the eleventh strophe of the later version, indicating that four strophes have been added to this section of the poem. The entire text comprises thirty-four strophes. The later *Ezzolied* falls into three roughly equal sections, the first devoted to the time from the Creation to Christ's birth, and the second to Christ's life on earth; the third is a hymn to the miracle of salvation accomplished by Christ's death on the cross, rich in Old Testament prefiguration and allegorical elaboration. By far the largest part of the scholarship on the *Ezzolied* has exhausted itself trying to reconstruct the missing parts of the fragmentary original by selecting parts of the later version felt to be Ezzo's work. Unfortunately, consensus has not been achieved. Here we have offered each version as it is actually transmitted: the earlier fragment free of any speculative reconstruction; the later expansion in its entirety.

The versions differ not only in length but also in other ways, as can be seen by comparing the first two strophes of the earlier version with the corresponding three strophes (2–4) of the later one. They differ in genre. The earlier version, in which the strophes are of the same length, was meant to be sung, while the later version, in which each strophe is of different length, was probably not. They differ in their esthetic ideal. The earlier is balanced and restrained. The first two strophes, of equal length, are devoted to the Old and the New Testaments respectively; this contrast comes to a point in the concluding lines, which are identical except for the very last word: in the first it is *eron*, the "glory" of the Old Testament; in the second it is *gnadon*, the "grace" of the New. The later version is expansive and didactic: two strophes have grown to three; lines have been added admonishing us to glorify the Lord and keep the Sabbath (4.6–10). The two versions differ in thematic emphasis, the earlier placing more weight on the typological relation of Old and New Testaments, the later on the grace promised by the New. The later version takes the first strophe of the earlier version, which had been devoted to the Old Testament, and infuses it with the New: the last word is no longer "glory" but "grace" (2.8), which has slipped in earlier as well (2.5). They envision different audiences. The earlier version expects an audience that is aristocratic, addressing itself in the very first line to *iu herron*, "you lords," while the later version, addressing itself to *iu allen*, "all of you" (2.1), seems to have a more general audience in mind. The earlier version is a song in praise of salvation addressed to a noble audience presumed to possess the intellectual background to appreciate its learned restraint. The later version is an expansive rhymed sermon addressed to all and placing greater stress on the hope of grace.

The *Annolied* appears at first glance to be a life of Anno von Steuß-lingen, archbishop of Cologne from 1056 until his death in 1075. But it is actually something more and different. It falls into three parts. After a prologue strophe, the first section (strophes 2–7) offers a condensed salvation history: the Creation, Fall, Incarnation, and Crucifixion are recorded; the apostles are sent out into the world; saints and martyrs are dispatched to Cologne where they establish a tradition that culminates in St. Anno. The second section (8–33) presents world history: the beginning of cities is followed by four empires; the strophes on Rome, which gets most of the attention, are monopolized by Caesar and particularly by his relations with the German tribes; the rule of Augustus leads to the birth of Christ; Peter converts Rome and dispatches missionaries to Cologne, who, as bishops, establish the line that culminates in Anno. The third section (34–49) is devoted entirely to Anno, but rather than a standard narrative saint's life, it offers selected snapshots: his works of charity, his power as regent for the underage emperor Henry IV, his tribulations, a vision, his death, and a posthumous miracle. The *Annolied* is clearly concerned to promote the figure of Anno, perhaps to improve his reputation among the people of Cologne, perhaps to further the effort to have him canonized. But it is also devoted to the empire, recounting its origin, elaborating the role of Caesar, particularly his relation to German tribes, and expressing anguish at the toll taken by the Investiture Controversy. Cities, particularly Cologne, are another thematic focus: the first two sections culminate in Cologne; the second begins with an account of the "origin of cities" (8.2); the German episcopal sees are traced back to their Roman foundation. The *Annolied* is a thematically complex and, as will become clearer below, carefully constructed work that packs an immense amount into a relatively small compass: classical and Christian learning, ancient and modern history, imperial, national and local politics.

Unfortunately, we have little certain information about its composition. Based on the historical events it mentions and its relation to other texts, one assumes it was written between 1077 and 1101. The author is unknown. It may have been written in Cologne, which figures prominently in the poem, or, more likely, in the nearby monastery at Siegburg, which had been established by Anno and which was the site of his grave. The monastery at Siegburg was without equal in the region as a scholarly and literary center and had a vested interest in promoting the reputation of the bishop who was interred there. No manuscripts of the *Annolied* survive, and we would not know of the text at all were it not for the efforts of two early modern scholars, the Dutch humanist Bonaventura Vulcanius, who published lines 2.1–5.4 in 1597, and the great poet and poetician Martin Opitz, who published the complete text — with a Latin preface and commentary — in 1639.

While the *Annolied* does not seem to have been well known in the Middle Ages, about 250 lines received wide circulation since they were adapted and incorporated into the *Kaiserchronik*, or *Chronicle of the Emperors*, a text that enjoyed considerable popularity. It was written in Regensburg by one or more anonymous authors, perhaps begir.ning as early as 1126 but more likely closer to 1150. A copy of the *Annolied* may have been in the possession of Kuno, who had been abbot of the monastery at Siegburg before becoming bishop of Regensburg (1126–32) and who may have brought the text with him when he journeyed south to assume his episcopal duties. If the *Annolied* is the first text to exploit the learned tradition of secular history for vernacular writing, but still coupled with salvation history, the *Kaiserchronik* was the first to abandon the salvation-historical framework and let secular history stand on its own. The *Kaiserchronik* is a chronicle of *emperors*, beginning with Caesar (not with Augustus and the birth of Christ) and continuing into the twelfth century. It seems to have filled a need for the German elite, since it was copied many times, continuations were written to bring it up to date, it was translated into Latin and adapted into German prose.

Whereas the *Kaiserchronik* usually abbreviates the material it takes from its sources, it expands what it has from the *Annolied*. It magnifies Caesar's opponents, German and Roman, thereby increasing the glory of the empire that can defeat them. It has a good deal more to say about the foundation of the cities on the Rhine and the battles around Trier, thereby adding information on specifically German history. It also changes the treatment of the dream in which the prophet Daniel sees four beasts proceed from the sea. While the *Annolied* takes the beasts to represent four empires, in the *Kaiserchronik* the beasts represent emperors, the third being Caesar. The focus is now on Caesar and his establishment of the Roman empire as a fulfillment of Old Testament prophecy. Each of the changes the *Kaiserchronik* makes to the text it adopts from the *Annolied* serves to magnify the empire and Germany.

Unlike the *Ezzolied* and the *Annolied*, each of the remaining texts in this volume is transmitted in only one version. All are anonymous, and all must have been written before the last quarter of the twelfth century, when they were incorporated into the Vorau manuscript, Cod. 276, the single manuscript in which they are found. Otherwise nothing is known about the circumstances of their composition. The *Lob Salomons* is made up of a series of scenes whose function is more iconic than narrative. The two principal scenes are in the center: the construction of the Temple, including the story of a dragon that directed Solomon to the tool that enables him to build the edifice without iron; and the visit of the Queen of Sheba, which provides an opportunity to describe various elements of Solomon's magnificent court. The central scenes are preceded by a brief account of how Solomon, offered the choice between riches and wisdom, chose wisdom and are followed by praise of Solomon as prince of peace.

The *Historia Judith* comprises two parts that must originally have been separate poems, known to modern scholars as *Die drei Jünglinge im Feuerofen*, or *Three Youths in the Furnace*, and *Die ältere Judith*, or *Earlier Story of Judith* (so called to distinguish it from a longer, presumably later, apparently unrelated version of the Judith story, which follows immediately in the Vorau mansucript). They survive, however, only in the Vorau manuscript, where they appear as a single text with the title *Historia Judith*. In the first part, an Old Testament narrative has been recast as a story of Christian martyrs. Three youths come to Nebuchadnezzar and attempt to convert him from his idolatry to Christianity. They are thrown into an oven, miraculously saved from harm, and many witnesses convert. In the second part, an Old Testament narrative has been recast as a heroic lay. The heathen general Holofernes, besieging Bethany, is attracted to the pious Judith and marries her. She gets him drunk at the wedding feast, prays while he sleeps, and receives instruction from an angel to cut off Holofernes's head and return to the city. The text breaks off here. The occasion for joining these two otherwise unrelated stories may have been the name Nebuchadnezzar, which belongs both to the Babylonian king who attempts to kill the youths and to the Assyrian king who dispatches his general, Holofernes, to destroy the Jews. The connection between the two is strengthened by the inclusion in the second section of six lines from the first (5.11–16, 13.3–8). Although these lines make little sense in their new context, they do introduce the name Nebuchadnezzar into the story of Judith. If Nebuchadnezzar is the common element, then the *Historia Judith* presents two episodes from the story of an impious and unjust king.

Although the texts that are translated in this volume were written at different times and places and for different purposes, all of them appear, in one form or another, in the largest and most important collection of early MHG texts, the famous Vorau manuscript, Cod. 276. The manuscript was written in the last quarter of the twelfth century, possibly in Regensburg or in Vorau itself. It begins with a large historical text, the *Kaiserchronik*, including, of course, that section adapted from the *Annolied*. A series of texts mostly on Old Testament themes follows, beginning with German versions of Genesis and Exodus and including the *Lob Salomons* and the *Historia Judith*. The end of this section is marked by a second historical text, Pfaffe Lambrecht's *Alexanderlied*, in its proper chronological position. This is followed by a series of texts on New Testament themes, including the later, expanded version of the *Ezzolied* and ending with an allegorical description of the Heavenly Jerusalem and prayers. The Vorau manuscript combines secular and religious texts in a salvation-historical framework, stretching from the Creation to the Last Judgment.

Since the Vorau manuscript contains the latest extant version of all the texts in this volume (except the *Kaiserchronik*), it offers evidence for the process of revision and appropriation by which older texts were adapted for a new context. It contains the later, expanded version of the *Ezzolied*, written sixty years after the first with different thematic emphases and addressed to a different audience. It contains the part of the *Annolied* that had been selected and adapted for inclusion, decades after its original composition, in the *Kaiserchronik*. In the *Historia Judith* the scribe has copied out two texts that must originally have been independent, but are now joined together, given a single title and thus a new meaning. In each case older texts have been preserved but at the same time changed in important ways to accommodate different contexts of reception. This "productive reception" is a sign of the value attached to the older texts: they are not discarded and replaced but re-produced and reused.

In the process, they are also used up. With the exception of the *Kaiserchronik*, each of the texts in this volume is transmitted in only a single manuscript. And, again with the exception of the *Kaiserchronik*, the Vorau manuscript represents the last time that any of the texts in this volume was copied. Although the reuse of the early MHG texts suggests that they were valued, they appear to have lost their value at the end of the twelfth century, when the fashion for secular texts based on French models swept over Germany. This fashion was establishing itself in the western regions in precisely those decades when the Vorau manuscript was being compiled in the east. Indeed, the Vorau manuscript did not remain untouched by this new vogue. In Pfaffe Lambrecht's *Alexanderlied* it has included the first German narrative to be based on a French source, the harbinger of things to come.

The Vorau manuscript provides a convenient summing up of the early MHG corpus. It is organized to highlight the two paramount themes: salvation history and secular sovereignty, particularly the history of the empire. It illustrates the "productive reception" of early MHG writing: texts first written 50 –125 years earlier are included, but in later adaptations or as part of later texts. And it marks a chronological boundary: the scribe who copied out the religious texts in the Vorau manuscript was the last to have shown any interest in preserving them. The future lay not with the religious texts but with the secular ones, the *Kaiserchronik* and Lambrecht's *Alexanderlied*, which continued to be copied and adapted. When the composition of religious texts in German begins again in earnest in the thirteenth century, it does so without reference to the impressive achievements of the eleventh and early twelfth centuries.

LATIN LEARNING AND VERNACULAR POETRY

Since the writers of the texts in this volume were highly educated clerics, it is hardly surprising that they are completely at home in the Latin learning of their age. What is remarkable is the extent to which they incorporate this learning into vernacular texts. Naturally, they draw on Scripture. Biblical narratives form the basis of the *Lob Salomons* (1 Kings 2–10; 2 Chronicles 1–9) and the *Historia Judith* (Daniel 3; Judith). Biblical references and citations appear at every turn, some of them in Latin: "Antiquus dierum" in the later *Ezzolied* (17.1) is from Daniel (7.9, 13, 22); *Lob Salomons* line 22.10 is a partial translation of Psalm 115.17; *Annolied* 44.6 is a German version of Job 2.7. The early MHG writers are also familiar with apocryphal traditions. Some of these are widely known, like the Harrowing of Hell, from the apocryphal Gospel of Nicodemus (*Annolied* 4.9–11; implied in the later *Ezzolied* 23.1–4). Others are less familiar, like the story of the dragon in the *Lob Salomons* (6–9), ultimately of Talmudic origin.

Just as important are traditions of biblical exegesis. When the later *Ezzolied* states that "God in his might creates a great multiplicity of signs" (5.1–2) it invokes a fundamental principle of medieval hermeneutics: that God, having created these signs, expects us to read them, and that if we do so correctly, we will discover other, true, allegorical significations. After describing the splendors of Solomon's court, the *Lob Salomons* offers such an allegorical reading: it tells us that Solomon "signifies God" (20.1), that the queen who visits him "signifies *ecclesia*" (21.2), and that Solomon's servants "signify bishops" (22.2). Both the *Ezzolied* and the *Annolied* understand that Moses leading the Israelites out of Egypt into the Promised Land "signifies that which is Christian" (later *Ezzolied*, 28.1): Christ leading the faithful "gently and swiftly into the blessed land of paradise" (*Annolied*, 49.25–26).

A related exegetical tradition sees a typological relation between figures and events of the Old Testament and those of the New. Old Testament events "prefigure" their New Testament "fulfillment." Since the one who comes from Bozrah about whom Isaiah asks (Isaiah 63.1–2) was believed to prefigure Christ, the later *Ezzolied* can state that the risen Christ simply *is* "the lord who came out of Bozrah" (24.1–2). The writers expect their audiences to be familiar with these traditions. Only if one knows that Solomon prefigures Christ and that a dragon can signify the devil can one appreciate what it means for Solomon to defeat the dragon in the *Lob Salomons*. Only if one knows the tree in the Garden of Eden prefigures the Cross can one have any idea what the later *Ezzolied* means when it claims: "Death arose from a tree. By a tree it was defeated" (21.9–10). Much of the power of the end of the *Ezzolied* results from way the poet piles sign upon sign, each of which "signifies" richly according to established allegorical and typological conventions.

While the Bible and its interpretation provide the basis, other learned traditions figure as well in the early MHG texts. The *Ezzolied* is infused by the *logos/lux/vita* theology that developed out of the gospel of John. The *Annolied* claims that "all creation" (the macrocosm) "is contained in humankind" (the microcosm) (2.12), a teaching of the Greek Church Fathers transmitted to the Latin West by John Scotus Eriugena. The later *Ezzolied* offers a variant of this idea that can be found from India to Ireland, and from ancient Greece to Slavic literatures, according to which the various parts of a human being were created out of various specific elements: stones become bones, grass becomes hair (5). Historical texts draw on historical sources. The *Kaiserchronik* is indebted to a medieval chronicle, the *Gesta Trevrorum* (which itself took from the *Annolied*!) for the material it adds on the history of the cities on the Rhine and the battles around Trier. The *Annolied* poet draws on the *Historia de preliis*, a tenth-century adaptation of a late-classical account of Alexander's life, for his representation of Alexander (14–15), on Virgil for his treatment of the Greeks and Trojans (22–23), and on Lucan both for his information about the conflict between Caesar and Pompey (25–27) and for the precise metaphors which he uses to characterize eleventh-century battles (*Annolied* 40.13–16 translates *Pharsalia* 1.2f.).

Although the texts in this volume will strike many modern readers as poorly organized, that is only because they are organized according to criteria that are no longer familiar to us. These too are drawn from the learned traditions of the Middle Ages. The *Annolied* exploits a tradition of allegorical exegesis going back to Jerome, according to which the four animals that the prophet Daniel sees in a dream (Daniel 7.1–28) represent the Babylonian, Persian, Macedonian, and Roman empires. The dream provides the framework for telling the histories of those four empires (12–33), each of which is introduced with a description of its signifying animal. Not only that: within the story of Rome, the dream also provides the framework for recounting Caesar's conquest of the German tribes. More or less explicit markers indicate that each tribe corresponds to one of the empires identified by Jerome: the Swabians to the Babylonians (19.9–13 hints back to 12.5–6); the Bavarians to the Persians (20.15–18: Armenia was believed to lie in Persia); the Saxons to the Greeks (21.5–8); and the Franks to the Romans (22.1–23.24). Ideologically this use of Daniel's dream represents what we would consider secular history as the fulfillment of biblical prophesy. Structurally the dream allegory organizes nearly half of the *Annolied*.

Both the *Ezzolied* and the *Annolied* rely on Christian number symbolism to provide overall coherence. The *Ezzolied*, in its later version, comprises 34 strophes — which is appropriate because, as the text itself reminds us, Christ "lived among us thirty-three years . . . and half of the thirty-fourth" (20.9–11). The *Annolied* ignores the half year and highlights thirty-three, also seven (days of creation, deadly sins, gifts of the Holy Ghost). The first section of the poem, devoted to salvation history, ends in strophe seven. The second section, devoted to world history, ends with strophe thirty-three. The third section, devoted to Anno's life, concludes with strophe seven-times-seven: forty-nine. These numbers have not only a general but also a particular significance. Anno was the thirty-third bishop and the seventh *saint* bishop of Cologne — as we are told in the thirty-third strophe!

While the texts in this volume participate in a sophisticated universe of Latin Christian learning, the language in which they are written was not Latin but German. We call this language Middle High German, and, since the term helps define this TEAMS series, perhaps some words are in order on what it means. Middle High German differs most noticeably from its predecessor, Old High German, in that the older language employs the full series of vowels in its inflectional endings, while MHG allows only *e*. Conveniently for purposes of illustration, the earlier *Ezzolied* has retained some of the older forms: verbs like *mahti* (4.8), *richeson* (5.10), and *lerta* (7.5); nouns like *eron* (4.11) and *hello* (5.11). The later *Ezzolied* modernizes these into the forms one would expect to find in a MHG text: *mohte*

(7.8), *richesen* (9.10), and *lert(e)* (11.5); *eren* (7.11) and *helle* (9.11). That the texts are not yet modern New High German is most obvious in that they have not yet undergone two vowel changes that distinguish these two stages of the language. They exhibit a series of long vowels (*i, u, ü*; conventionally spelled *î, û, iu*) that have since become diphthongs (*ei, au, eu*). The *Kaiserchronik*, for example has MHG *Rîn* (375) rather than modern *Rhein, sû* (372) instead of *Sau*, and *Diuze* (381; the *iu* is long *ü*) rather than *Deutz*. At the same time they retain a series of diphthongs (*ie, uo*, and *üe* — often spelled *uo*) that are now long vowels (*i, u,* and *ü*). The *Kaiserchronik* has *vier* (330), which we still spell the same way, although we now pronounce *ie* as long *i, fuoren* (332) which has become *fuhren*, and *kuonen* (364; this *uo* is actually *üe*), which would now be *kühnen.*

Although the texts in this volume are among the first to have been written in MHG and although their composition stretches over nearly a century, they are shaped by a remarkably coherent poetics, one quite different from that which is found in the better-known texts written in the decades around 1200. The basic metrical unit of the early MHG texts is the four-stress line. Yet it is treated very casually: in close proximity, the *Historia Judith* offers a line of six syllables, which is most naturally read with only two stresses (6.10), and another of seventeen syllables, which reads easily as a nine-stress line (5.16). The lines are rhymed as couplets, yet here too the effect is remarkably casual since assonance is accepted along with pure rhyme. Of the nine rhymes in the magnificent first strophe of the *Annolied,* only three are pure. In every text except the *Kaiserchronik*, the rhymed couplets are grouped together into strophes. The term is used rather loosely, since, except in the earlier *Ezzolied*, the strophes within each text vary considerably in length. Nevertheless, these "strophes" were clearly meaningful units to those who composed and copied them. The writers of the later *Ezzolied* and the *Annolied* rely on the division into strophes for their number symbolism. The scribes who copied the texts into the surviving manuscripts preserve the division into strophes, marking the beginning of each with an initial.

The most striking stylistic feature of these texts is their pervasive parataxis. In the first strophe of the later *Ezzolied*, only two clauses are connected through the grammatical subordination of one to another (hypotaxis) — lines 5 and 6 by *want*, "because," and lines 9 and 10 by *duo*, "when" or "then." Otherwise the strophe comprises a series of short, independent clauses (parataxis). Since each clause is the length of a line or a couplet, syntactic and poetic boundaries reinforce one another. The absence of explicit connections also occurs *within* a sentence (asyndeton). The first line of the strophe, *Der guote biscoph Guntere vone Babenberch*, stands in apposition, but without any grammatical connection, to the first word of the second line, the subject of the sentence, *der* (literally: "The noble bishop Gunther of Bamberg, *he* commissioned . . ."). The prevalence of parataxis and asyndeton and the predominance of sentences that are just as long as a line or a couplet give the early MHG texts their fundamental stylistic character. They are built up of a series of small, independent units (clauses, lines, couplets) that stand next to each other but that do not stand in any explicit causal, grammatical, or logical relation to one another. The relations among these small pieces are implicit and spatial rather than explicit and grammatical. In translating I have tried to preserve this character by resisting the temptation to add conjunctions and thereby create longer, more complex sentences than exist in the original.

Not only do these texts avoid complex sentences; they also disdain elaborate ornament. Nouns ordinarily appear without attributive adjectives or genitive modifiers. Compound nouns are rare. The seventy-six lines of the earlier *Ezzolied* contain eighty German nouns, not one of them a compound. Only five are modified by attributive adjectives. This reticence heightens the significance of those adjectives that do occur. *War*, "true," appears three times: it imbues both the "true account" Ezzo promises to give (1.2) and the light metaphors to which he is devoted — God's son is the "true sun" (6.12) — with the unassailable truth of the "true God" (3.1). Similarly, because compound nouns (and adjectives) are so rare, those that do appear carry more weight than they otherwise might. Ezzo creates compounds that, although few, are particularly striking: *nebilvinster* (6.8), "mist-dark"; and in the later version *werltwuostunge* (12.10), "world-desert," and *nagelgebente* (21.2), "nail-bonds."

This is not to say that the poets eschewed all ornament. But the poetic figures they favored are those congenial to the basic style of the texts: alliteration, anaphora, lists, and parallel structures. The first strophe of the *Annolied* begins with the alliteration of *dikke* and *dingen* in the first two lines and of *burge brêchen* in line 4. Lines 3–6 are joined by anaphora, each line beginning with the same word, *wî*, "how." These same lines also comprise a list, a list of features that amounts to a definition of Germanic heroic poetry. The lines also share a parallel structure: each begins with *wî*, and each ends with a verb. Other forms of repetition also occur: in the *Lob Salomons* strophes 15 and 16 begin with the same line, 7 and 9 with nearly the same line. Alliteration, anaphora, lists, parallel structures, and other forms of repetition establish connections between words or clauses that are aural and spatial rather than semantic, grammatical, or logical. As such they are in harmony with the basic paratactic, asyndetic structure of the verse, which, similarly, fosters implicit, spatial relations.

As highly educated clerics, the authors of the texts in this volume were certainly familiar with ways of writing in Latin that are syntactically complex and highly ornamented. Occasionally they will produce something similar — like the sentence that takes up most of the pivotal strophe 7 of the *Annolied*, which represents *syntactically* the reciprocal relation of Anno and Cologne. Writers can produce such sentences. But, with rare exceptions, they prefer a quite different stylistic ideal. That ideal is not musical or painterly but architectural. Its power comes from the static arrangement of compact blocks, each one laden with meaning, and from the effective use of a small number of devices. It is more likely to inspire awe than delight. As a consequence the early MHG texts have a much different feel from the more familiar works written around 1200, with their pure rhymes and polished meter, their longer periods, flexible syntax, and delight in artifice. However, the early MHG style is not an imperfect forerunner of Gottfried and Wolfram. It is a coherent and effective style in its own right.

This style resonates with the long tradition of oral poetry in German and seems also to be connected with a pride in things German. The opening lines of the *Annolied*, "We have often heard songs about events of old," recall the beginning of heroic poems like the *Hildebrandslied* and the *Nibelungenlied*, where the singer steps forth as the voice of a shared tradition. The second part of the *Historia Judith* condenses the Old Testament story of Judith into something like a heroic lay. The fondness for alliteration and the division into strophes, although possible in Latin verse, of course, invoke even more strongly the Germanic heroic tradition: the *Hildebrandslied*, like older Germanic verse, does not use end rhyme but alliteration as its principle of sonic organization; the *Nibelungenlied*, like many heroic epics (but unlike romances and most religious texts), is divided into strophes.

The texts reveal a growing awareness of and pride in belonging to a larger collective of Germans. The *Annolied* celebrates the (otherwise unattested) role that the German tribes played in Caesar's victories. The *Kaiserchronik* adds even more material on Germany to the passage it took from the *Annolied*. The *Annolied* is the earliest text in which *diutsch*, "German," is used to refer to something other than language: formulations like "on German soil" (7.4) and "German men" (28.17) suggest an awareness of a commonality that embraces the various tribes — although it still must compete with the poet's shameless pride in everything Frankish. And people were pleased with what was accomplished in German. The prologue strophe to the later *Ezzolied* contains only one adjective, *guot*, "good," "noble," "pious"; it appears three times in the first four lines, joining together in praise Gunther, the "noble bishop of Bamberg" and the "most excellent work" that he commissioned. The writer of the *Vita Altmanni* also has praise for Ezzo, who is said to have composed his song *nobiliter*, "nobly," "elegantly" in his native language.

The writers of the early MHG texts drew on venerable traditions of theological and historical learning accessible only to those who were themselves educated and could read the Latin in which this learning was transmitted. They drew broadly on this material, combined elements freely to suit their purposes, and expressed them in German verse that, although simple in some ways, is nevertheless capable of great power and that, although it refers to the tradition of oral heroic poetry, is nevertheless clearly conceived as a written form. This synthesis is the decisive step that stands at the beginning of the continuous history of German literature.

CHURCH AND EMPIRE, CULTURE AND POWER

The information we have about the composition of the *Ezzolied* allows us to say something about the cultural context in which this step was taken. Gunther of Bamberg, who commissioned the *Ezzolied*, was born into the high nobility and had served the emperor Henry III as imperial chancellor in Italy before being appointed bishop of Bamberg in 1057. In 1064 he led the first great pilgrimage to the Holy Land from German soil, dying in 1065 on the return trip, shortly before he would have reached home. He was cosmopolitan, highly educated, and open to the intellectual currents of his day. He seems to have been sympathetic to church reform, since he reorganized the cathedral chapter and established a much stricter regulation of the canons' life. He also seems to have liked to listen to German heroic tales: Meinhard, head of the cathedral school, criticizes him in a letter for always thinking of Attila and Dietrich von Bern rather than of Augustine and Gregory.

The school at Bamberg had been founded by Henry II in 1007 and was one of the leading intellectual centers in eleventh-century Germany. Meinhard, who taught at the school from around 1060 until 1085, when he became bishop of Würzburg, was one of the great Latin stylists of his generation. His letters are a rich source of information for historians of the period. Many of those associated with the school went on to occupy imperial offices or important episcopal sees. Anno, for instance, had been a scholar in Bamberg before becoming chaplain in the imperial chapel and then archbishop of Cologne. Ezzo and Anno are not the only figures associated with the cathedral school to figure prominently in the history of German literature. Just about the time Ezzo composed his song, a commentary on the Song of Songs in German prose heavily mixed with Latin was written by Williram, who was in Bamberg between about 1040 and 1048, when he became abbot at Ebersberg.

Gunther and those around him combined in their persons noble birth, political and ecclesiastical power, Latin learning, and an interest in German poetry. This is the context in which the decisive step was taken, in which the learned traditions of the high Middle Ages were joined with the quite different traditions of German verse for the first time, to create one of the great religious poems of the age. The context also explains other features of the *Ezzolied*. It explains the theological learning that Ezzo assumes on the part of his audience. It explains why he addressed his song, explicitly, to nobles (1.1). It also explains the relation that Ezzo expects between God and humanity. Christ, according to Ezzo, does not teach love, fear, or renunciation of the world, but rather "humility and proper behavior, . . . loyalty and truth" (later version, 20.3–4). He teaches the virtues a lord would expect from his vassal (see also *Annolied*, 4.13). In return, the vassal can expect certain things from his lord — which explains the assurance with which the poet can exhort God to *keep* his promise, to "fulfill your words" and "draw us up to you" (later version, 32.8, 32.6). The *Ezzolied* expresses the great confidence of those, secure in their high station, who see no contradiction between the power they enjoy in this world and the salvation they expect in the next, nor between the German poetry of the secular court and the Latin learning of the cathedral school.

Like Gunther, Anno von Steußlingen was a churchman who wielded great secular power. As noted, he had been associated with the cathedral school in Bamberg until he was called to the imperial chapel in Goslar. In 1056 Henry III named Anno archbishop of Cologne (*Annolied*, 34.5–20), which made him not only spiritual but also secular lord of the city and thus one of the most powerful figures in the empire. After Henry's death, Anno led a group of nobles who opposed the regency of Agnes, Henry's widow. In the spring of 1062 they lured the future Henry IV, then twelve years old, onto a ship and, along with the royal insignia, carried him off to Cologne. Anno assumed guardianship of Henry and acted as regent until 1064 (*Annolied*, 37.1–10). Anno greatly increased the revenues and possessions of his diocese, fostered the construction of churches, founded monasteries, and introduced a strict observance of the rule into those religious houses under his jurisdiction. His relations with the people of Cologne, however, were not always peaceful. In 1074 he commandeered a ship so that the bishop of Münster could return home and, in the ensuing turmoil, the bishop's residence was stormed and Anno had to flee the city. Three days later he returned with an army and took revenge on his flock that is said to have cost several hundred lives. Not until a year later did he make peace with the citizens (*Annolied*, 43.23). Shortly thereafter he withdrew to the monastery at Siegburg, where he died after a painful illness in 1076. He was canonized in 1183. The mixture of sacred and secular, learning and action, piety and ruthlessness that characterizes the life of Anno is nicely summed up in the inscription on his episcopal staff, which combines Virgil (*Eclogues*, 3.20) with Scripture (Matthew 10.16, 15.14; Luke 6.39): "Tityrus, govern your flock. Lead them not as the blind leads the blind. Be austere in your behavior, but learn to be a gentle ruler. Protect the simplicity of the mourning dove with the cunning of the serpent" (Arnold, 113).

Like the *Ezzolied*, the *Annolied* is concerned with sovereignty and salvation. This dual focus is expressed in the summary that the text gives of its hero's career: "At the palace his power was so great that all the imperial princes sat below him. In the service of God he carried himself as if he were an angel. He preserved his good name in both camps" (34.15–19). In spite of the ease with which Anno wins praise "in both camps," the *Annolied* actually has a difficult time reconciling them. Unlike the *Ezzolied*, which proceeds smoothly from Creation to salvation, the *Annolied* puts salvation history first, then starts all over again with world history (8). On the one hand, world history is the fulfillment of the Old Testament prophecy in Daniel's dream. On the other, it is parallel to, rather than part of, salvation history. World history is full of strife, from Ninus, "the first man who ever started a war" (8.5–6), up to the "wretched struggle" during the reign of Henry IV, "when the empire was brought into confusion" (40.1, 40.3). Anno himself receives a "blemish" (43.7) from his conflict with the citizens of Cologne that puts his own salvation in jeopardy (42.20–22). The optimistic universalism of salvation history is difficult to reconcile with the series of particular calamities one finds in the world, both in the past and in the present. The solution seems to be individualistic: Anno acted rightly in his own particular situation; if we do the same, we too will be saved.

Unfortunately, we do not know enough about the composition of the other texts to connect them with assurance to any particular historical figure. Nevertheless, they too wrestle with issues of secular power and salvation. The *Lob Salomons* and the *Historia Judith* represent one possibility, texts that ignore the German present in favor of the biblical past. Yet they too are concerned with rulers who do or do not exercise their sovereignty in accordance with God's command. Placed next to one another in the Vorau manuscript, the two texts can be read as pendant portraits of the pious and just Solomon on the one hand, the impious and violent Nebuchadnezzar on the other. The *Kaiserchronik* represents a different possibility, a text that focuses on secular rather than biblical history. It follows a line of historical emperors from Caesar up into the twelfth century. And yet, although the *Kaiserchronik* is organized as secular history, each emperor is matched with a pope, the emperors are judged good or bad according to Christian standards, and the relation between the heathen Roman empire and the medieval Christian empire can be read as one of prefiguration and fulfillment. Although none of the later texts seems to have quite the confidence of the *Ezzolied*, and although each directs its focus differently to sacred or secular topics, all of them remain concerned with those same themes: sovereignty and salvation.

They were not the last. About the time the Vorau manuscript was being compiled, Hartmann von Aue was bringing the first German Arthurian romance, *Erec*, to a close with the assurance that his hero and heroine, having attained "the earthly crown," were rewarded "with eternal life" (10127–29). Several decades later Wolfram von Eschenbach concludes *Parzival* with the observation that it is "a useful effort" if someone can manage to "end his life so that God is not robbed of the soul on account of the sins of the flesh and who is nevertheless able to retain the favor of the world with dignity" (827.19–24). Like the writers of the texts in this volume, Hartmann and Wolfram do not see any contradiction between the pursuit of glory in this world and the hope of salvation in the next. Leading one's life so that "God is not robbed of the soul" need not deprive one of "the favor of the world." Indeed, the pursuit of "the earthly crown" is *justified* by the reward of "eternal life": by bestowing the latter, God grants his blessing to the former. Hartmann is not Ezzo, of course. The earlier writers are clerics writing from within church institutions — monasteries, cathedral schools, episcopal courts — for audiences that were steeped in the learning of the church; the later ones are educated knights writing at the courts of secular princes for audiences hungry for stories about King Arthur. The earlier writers drew on Augustine and Virgil, on the learned tradition of Latin theology and history; the later ones were more likely to turn to Ovid and Horace, to the less austere tradition of Latin poetry and poetics, and, of course, to Chrétien and the irresistible French romances. The earlier texts sought to justify sovereignty within the learned context of salvation history; the later ones seek to justify courtly culture in the context of lay piety.

Nevertheless, Hartmann and Wolfram are the direct descendants of Ezzo. They are heirs to a fusion of elements that was first achieved by Ezzo and the writers of the other early MHG texts. They united the Latin learning of the schools with a coherent and compelling written German verse style. And they united the conviction that the pursuit of earthly power and glory is good with the conviction that God would reward those who devote themselves to this pursuit. This new fusion of elements required not just an education in the Latin traditions and an interest in German poetry, but also the cultural and political status to enable and to legitimate a new kind of writing. It is hardly surprising that these texts represent and reflect on the combination of learning and power that enabled their production. Nor is it surprising that they exude confidence, a confidence founded on noble birth, great learning, the successful exercise of imperial and episcopal power, and the certainty of divine approval. Without such confidence, this new kind of writing might never have been attempted.

BIBLIOGRAPHY

This bibliography lists the works on which I have drawn or that are cited in the introduction. In addition it lists the editions of the MHG texts that are reprinted in this volume and all the relevant English-language literature of which I am aware. Those who wish to read further in German beyond the few articles and histories listed below should consult Gentry, *Bibliographie,* Ruh, *Verfasserlexikon,* and Haug/Vollmann, *Frühe deutsche Literatur,* for recent bibliographies on individual texts. Haug/Vollmann, which includes nearly all the texts in this volume, also contains excellent commentaries. The same is true of Nellmann's edition of the *Annolied.*

GENERAL WORKS

Batts, Michael. "Numbers and Number Symbolism in Medieval German Poetry." *Modern Language Quarterly* 24 (1963): 342–49.

Curschmann, Michael. "Middle High German Literature." In Strayer, *Dictionary of the Middle Ages,* 8:347–62.

de Boor, Helmut. "Frühmittelhochdeutscher Sprachstil." *Zeitschrift für deutsche Philologie* 51 (1926): 244–74, 52 (1927): 31–76.

Gentry, Francis G. *Bibliographie zur frühmittelhochdeutschen geistlichen Dichtung.* Bibliographien zur deutschen Literatur des Mittelalters, 11. Berlin: Schmidt, 1992.

Gentry, Francis G. "The Turn Toward the World: The Religious and Social Upheaval of the 11th Century and Early Middle High German Literature." In *Gesellschaftsgeschichte: Festschrift für Karl Bosl zum 80. Geburtstag,* ed. Ferdinand Seibt, 1: 45–51. Munich: Oldenbourg, 1988.

Gibbs, Marion E., and Sidney M. Johnson. *Medieval German Literature: A Companion.* New York: Garland, 1997.

Haug, Walter. *Vernacular Literary Theory in the Middle Ages: The German Tradition, 800–1300, in its European Context.* Trans. Joanna M. Catling. Cambridge Studies in Medieval Literature, 29. New York: Cambridge University Press, 1997.

Haug, Walter, and Benedikt Konrad Vollmann. *Frühe deutsche Literatur und lateinische Literatur in Deutschland 800–1150.* Bibliothek deutscher Klassiker, 62. Frankfurt am Main: Deutscher Klassiker Verlag, 1991.

Jaeger, C. Stephen. *The Envy of Angels: Cathedral Schools and Social Ideals in Medieval Europe, 950–1200.* Philadelphia: University of Pennsylvania Press, 1994.

Johnson, Sidney M. "Authorial Stance in Early Middle High German Religious Poetry." In *Semper idem et novus: Festschrift for Frank Banta*, ed. Francis G. Gentry, Göppinger Arbeiten zur Germanistik, 481, 231–46. Göppingen: Kümmerle, 1988.

Kartschoke, Dieter. *Geschichte der deutschen Literatur im frühen Mittelalter.* Munich: Deutscher Taschenbuch Verlag, 1990.

Kuhn, Hugo. "Frühmittelhochdeutsche Literatur." In *Reallexikon der deutschen Literaturgeschichte*, ed. Paul Merker and Wolfgang Stammler, 2nd ed. Werner Kohlschmidt and Wolfgang Mohr, 1:494–507. Berlin: de Gruyter, 1958.

———. "Gestalten und Lebenskräfte der frühmittelhochdeutschen Dichtung: Ezzos Lied, Genesis, Annolied, Memento mori." In Hugo Kuhn, *Dichtung und Welt im Mittelalter*, 2nd ed., 112–32. Stuttgart: Metzler, 1969.

Ruh, Kurt, with Gundolf Keil, Werner Schröder, Burghart Wachinger, and Franz Josef Worstbrock, eds. *Die deutsche Literatur des Mittelalters: Verfasserlexikon.* 2nd ed. Berlin: de Gruyter, 1978–.

Strayer, Joseph R., ed. *Dictionary of the Middle Ages.* 13 vols. New York: Scribner, 1982–89.

Vollmann-Profe, Gisela. *Wiederbeginn volkssprachiger Schriftlichkeit im hohen Mittelalter (1050/60–1160/70). Geschichte der deutschen Literatur von den Anfängen bis zum Beginn der Neuzeit*, ed. Joachim Heinzle, 1.2. Königstein/Ts.: Athenäum, 1986.

INDIVIDUAL MHG TEXTS

ANNOLIED

MHG Text: *Das Annolied: Mittelhochdeutsch und Neuhochdeutsch.* Ed., trans., commentary by Eberhard Nellmann. Universal-Bibliothek, 1416. Stuttgart: Reclam, 1979.

Arnold, Benjamin. "From Warfare on Earth to Eternal Paradise: Archbishop Anno II of Cologne, the History of the Western Empire in the *Annolied,* and the Salvation of Mankind." *Viator* 23 (1992): 95–113.

Batts, Michael. "On the Form of the Annolied." *Monatshefte* 52 (1960): 179–82.

Gellinek, Christian. "Daniel's Vision of Four Beasts in Twelfth-Century German Literature." *Germanic Review* 41 (1966): 5–26 [*Annolied*, 9–14].

Monumenta Annonis: Köln und Siegburg: Weltbild und Kunst im hohen Mittelalter: Eine Ausstellung des Schnütgen-Museums der Stadt Köln in der Cäcilienkirche vom 30. April bis zum 27. Juli 1975. Ed. Anton Legner. Cologne: Greven & Bechtold, 1975.

Whitesell, Frederick R. "Martin Opitz' Edition of the Annolied." *Journal of English and Germanic Philology* 43 (1944): 16–22.

EZZOLIED

MHG Text: "Ezzos Cantilena de miraculis Christi." In Werner Schröder, ed., *Kleinere deutsche Gedichte des 11. und 12. Jahrhunderts*, 1:1–26. Altdeutsche Textbibliothek, 71. Tübingen: Niemeyer, 1972.

Freytag, Hartmut. "Ezzos Gesang: Text und Funktion." In *Geistliche Denkformen in der Literatur des Mittelalters*, ed. Klaus Grubmüller, Ruth Schmidt-Wiegand, Klaus Speckenbach, 154–70. Münstersche Mittelalter-Schriften, 51. Munich: Fink, 1984.

Marchand, James W. "The Ship Allegory in the *Ezzolied* and in Old Icelandic." *Neophilologus* 60 (1976): 238–250.

Rupp, Heinz. "Ezzos 'Cantilena de miraculis Christi.'" In Heinz Rupp, *Deutsche religiöse Dichtungen des 11. und 12. Jahrhunderts: Untersuchungen und Interpretationen*, 2nd ed., 33–83. Bern: Francke, 1971.

Urbanek, Ferdinand. "Das Ezzolied in den Traditionen der Redekunst." *Zeitschrift für deutsche Philologie* 106 (1987): 321–40, 107 (1988): 26–48.

HARTMANN VON AUE

Hartmann von Aue. *Erec*. Ed. Albert Leitzmann and Ludwig Wolff, 6th ed. Christoph Cormeau and Kurt Gärtner. Altdeutsche Textbibliothek, 39. Tübingen: Niemeyer, 1985.

HISTORIA JUDITH

MHG Text: "Die drei Jünglinge im Feuerofen," "Die Ältere Judith." In Werner Schröder, ed., *Kleinere deutsche Gedichte des 11. und 12. Jahrhunderts*, 1:56–67. Altdeutsche Textbibliothek, 71. Tübingen: Niemeyer, 1972.

KAISERCHRONIK

MHG Text: *Die Kaiserchronik eines Regensburger Geistlichen.* Ed. Edward Schröder. Monumenta Germaniae historica, Deutsche Chroniken und andere Geschichtsbücher des Mittelalters, 1.1. Hannover: Hahn, 1892. Reprint. Dublin: Weidmann, 1964.

Gellinek, Christian. "Daniel's Vision of Four Beasts in Twelfth-Century German Literature." *Germanic Review* 41 (1966): 5–26 [*Kaiserchronik*, 14–20].

Mergell, Bodo. "Annolied und Kaiserchronik." *Beiträge zur Geschichte der deutschen Sprache und Literatur* (Halle) 77 (1955): 124–46.

Ohly, Ernst Friedrich. *Sage und Legende in der Kaiserchronik: Untersuchungen über Quellen und Aufbau der Dichtung*. Forschungen zur deutschen Sprache und Dichtung, 10. Münster: Aschendorff, 1940. Reprint. Darmstadt: Wissenschaftliche Buchgesellschaft, 1968.

LOB SALOMONS

MHG Text: "Das Lob Salomons." In Werner Schröder, ed., *Kleinere deutsche Gedichte des 11. und 12. Jahrhunderts*, 1:43–55. Altdeutsche Textbibliothek, 71. Tübingen: Niemeyer, 1972.

Curschmann, Michael. "Texte — Bilder — Strukturen: Der *Hortus deliciarum* und die frühmittelhochdeutsche Geistlichendichtung." *Deutsche Vierteljahrsschrift für Literaturwissenschaft und Geistesgeschichte* 55 (1981): 379–418.

Ganz, P[eter] F. "On the Unity of the Middle High German *Lob Salomons*. In *Mediaeval German Studies Presented to Frederick Norman*, 46–59. London: University of London, Institute of Germanic Studies, 1965.

Halperin, David J. "The *Book of Remedies,* the Canonization of the Solomonic Writings, and the Riddle of Pseudo-Eusebius." *Jewish Quarterly Review* 72 (1982): 269–92 [*Lob Salomons,* 285–87].

WOLFRAM VON ESCHENBACH

Wolfram von Eschenbach. *Parzival*. In *Wolfram von Eschenbach*, 1–3, ed. Albert Leitzmann, 6th ed. (vol. 2); 7th ed. (vol. 1 and 3) revised Wilhelm Deinert, Altdeutsche Textbibliothek, 12–14. Tübingen: Niemeyer, 1961, 1963, 1965.

TEXTS

DAS EZZOLIED

EZZO
CANTILENA DE MIRACULIS CHRISTI

Straßburg, Cod. germ. 278

1   Nu wil ih iu herron
        heina war reda vor tuon:
        von dem angenge,
        von alem manchunne,
   5   von dem wistuom alse manicvalt
        (ter an dien buchin stet gezalt)
        uzer genesi unde uzer libro regum,
        tirre werlte al ze dien eron.

2   Lux in tenebris,
        daz sament uns ist:
        der uns sin lieht gibit,
        neheiner untriwon er nefligit.
   5   in principio erat verbum,
        daz ist waro gotes sun;
        von einimo worte er bechom
        dire werlte al ze dien gnadon.

3   Ware got, ih lobin dih,
        din anegenge gihen ih.
        taz anagenge bistu, trehten, ein
        (ih negiho in anderz nehein):
   5   der got tes himilis,
        wages unde luftes,
        unde tes in dien viern ist
        ligentes unde lebentes:
        daz geskuofe du allez eino,
  10 du nebedorftost helfo darzuo.

Ezzo's Song

Ezzo
A Song about the Miracles of Christ

earlier, fragmentary version from the Straßburg manuscript

1   I will now present to you,
      lords, a true account
      of the beginning,
      of all humankind,
  5 of the manifold wisdom
      that is recounted in Scripture,
      in *Genesis* and in *Liber Regum*,
      to the glory of all the world.

2   *Lux in tenebris*,
      which is among us,
      who bestows his light upon us,
      he never betrays his troth.
  5 *In principio erat verbum.*
      In truth, that is the son of God.
      By means of a word he bestowed
      grace on all the world.

3   True God, I praise you.
      I affirm you as the beginning.
      You alone, Lord, are the beginning.
      I profess no other one.
  5 Lord of heaven,
      of the sea and the air
      and of all things animate and inanimate
      that are within those four,
      you alone created all of this.
 10 You did not require any aid in doing so.

ih wil dih ze anegenge haben
in worten unde in werchen.

4   Got, tu gescuofe al daz ter ist;
ane dih ne ist nieht.
ze aller jungest gescuofe du den man
nah tinem bilde getan,
5   nah tiner getate,
taz er gewalt habete.
du blies imo dinen geist in,
taz er ewic mahti sin;
noh er nevorhta imo den tot,
10   ub er gehielte din gebot.
ze allen eron gescuofe du den man:
du wissos wol sinen val.

5   Wie der man getate,
tes gehugen wir leider note;
turh tes tiufeles rat
wie skier er ellende wart!
5   vil harto gie diu sin scult
uber alle sin afterchumft;
sie wurden allo gezalt
in des tiuveles gewalt.
vil mihil was tiu unser not:
10   to begonda richeson ter tot,
ter hello wuohs ter ir gewin,
manchunne al daz fuor dar in.

6   Do sih Adam do bevil,
do was naht unde vinster.
do skinen her in welte
die sternen be ir ziten,
5   die vil lucel liehtes paren,
so berhte so sie waren;
wanda sie beskatwota
diu nebilvinster naht,
tiu von demo tievele chom,
10   in des gewalt wir waren,

I will take you as my beginning
in word and in deed.

4   God, you created everything that there is.
       Without you there is nothing.
       Last of all you created man, shaped
       according to your own image,
5   according to your form,
       so that he might hold power.
       You breathed your spirit into him
       so that he might be eternal.
       Nor would he have to fear death
10   as long as he kept your commandment.
       You created man for the highest glory.
       You were well aware that he would fall.

5   Sadly, we must needs remember
       how man acted.
       How quickly he was cast out
       because he listened to the Devil's counsel!
5   The great weight of his guilt
       passed on to all his descendants.
       They were all given
       into the power of the Devil.
       Our misery was very great.
10   Then death began its reign.
       The winnings of hell increased.
       All humankind passed into it.

6   After Adam had fallen
       there was darkness and night.
       The stars shone into the world
       at their appointed times
5   but they yielded very little light,
       no matter how bright they were,
       since they were overshadowed
       by the dark mist of the night
       that came from the Devil,
10   in whose power we were

unz uns erskein der gotis sun,
ware sunno von den himelen.

7   Der sternen aller ielich,
ter teilet uns daz sin lieht.
sin lieht taz cab uns Abel,
taz wir durh reht ersterben.
5   do lerta uns Enoch,
daz unseriu werh sin al in got.
uzer der archo gab uns Noe
ze himile reht gedinge.
do lert uns Abraham,
10   daz wir gote sin gehorsam;
der vil guote David,
daz wir wider ubele

until the son of God appeared to us,
the true sun of the heavens.

7   Each and every one of the stars
bestows its light on us.
Abel gave us his light
so that we would die for righteousness's sake.
5   Later Enoch taught us
that all our works should be in God.
From the ark Noah gave us
true hope of heaven.
Then Abraham taught us
10   to obey God.
The most excellent David
that we . . . against evil

DAS EZZOLIED

EZZO
CANTILENA DE MIRACULIS CHRISTI

Vorau, Cod. 276

1   Der guote biscoph Guntere vone Babenberch,
      der hiez machen ein vil guot werch:
      er hiez die sine phaphen
      ein guot liet machen.
   5 eines liedes si begunden,
      want si di buoch chunden.
      Ezzo begunde scriben,
      Wille vant die wise.
      duo er die wise duo gewan,
  10 duo ilten si sich alle munechen.
      von ewen zuo den ewen
      got gnade ir aller sele.

2   Ich wil iu eben allen
      eine vil ware rede vor tuon:
      von dem minem sinne
      von dem rehten anegenge,
   5 von den genaden also manechvalt,
      di uns uz den buochen sint gezalt,
      uzzer genesi unt uz libro regum,
      der werlt al ze genaden.

3   Die rede di ich nu sol tuon,
      daz sint di vier ewangelia.
      in principio erat verbum,
      daz was der ware gotes sun:
   5 von dem einem worte
      er bequam ze troste aller dirre werlte.

Ezzo's Song

Ezzo
A Song about the Miracles of Christ

later, expanded version from the Vorau manuscript

1   Gunther, the noble bishop of Bamberg,
      commissioned a most excellent work.
      He told his clerics
      to create a good song.
    5 They began working on a song
      since they were familiar with Scripture.
      Ezzo wrote the text.
      Wille made up the tune.
      When he had completed the tune
  10 everyone hastened to become a monk.
      May God have mercy on their souls
      for all eternity.

2   I will now present all of you
      with a completely true account,
      from my own understanding,
      of the true beginning,
    5 of the manifold acts of grace
      that are recounted to us from Scripture,
      from *Genesis* and from *Liber Regum*,
      bringing grace to all the world.

3   The account that I will give now
      is the four gospels.
      In principio erat verbum.
      That was the true son of God.
    5 From that one word
      he came to comfort all the world.

4   O lux in tenebris,
        du herre, du der mit samet uns bist,
        du uns daz ware lieht gibest,
        neheiner untriwe du nephligist.
     5   du gæbe uns einen herren,
        den scholte wir vil wol eren.
        daz was der guote suntach,
        necheines werches er nephlach:
        du spræche, ube wir den behilten,
     10   wir paradyses gewilten.

5   Got mit siner gewalt,
        der wurchet zeichen vil manecvalt;
        der worhte den mennischen einen
        uzzen von aht teilen:
     5   von dem leime gab er ime daz fleisch,
        der tou becechenit den sweiz,
        von dem steine gab er ime daz pein
        (des nist zwivil nehein),
        von den wurcen gab er ime di adren,
     10   von dem grase gab er ime daz har,
        von dem mere gab er ime daz pluot,
        von den wolchen daz muot.
        duo habet er ime begunnen
        der ougen von der sunnen.
     15   er verleh ime sinen atem,
        daz wir ime den behilten,
        unte sinen gesin,
        daz wir ime imer wuocherente sin.

6   Warer got, ich lobe dich,
        ein anegenge gih ich ane dich.
        daz anegenge bistu, trehtin, ein
        (ja negih ich anderez nehein),
     5   der erde joch des himeles,
        wages unte luftes
        unt alles des in den vieren ist
        lebentes unte ligentes:
        daz geschuophe du allez eine,

4   *O lux in tenebris,*
     you, Lord, who are among us,
     you give us the true light.
     You never betray your troth.
5   You gave us a lord.
     We should glorify him greatly.
     On the holy day, Sunday,
     he performed no work.
     You said that if we observed the sabbath
10   we would attain paradise.

5   God in his might
     creates a great multiplicity of signs.
     He shaped a single human
     outwardly from eight materials.
5   From clay he gave him flesh.
     Dew signifies sweat.
     From stones he gave him bones.
     There is no doubt of this.
     From roots he gave him blood vessels.
10   From grass he gave him hair.
     From the sea he gave him blood.
     From the clouds, mind.
     Then he created eyes for him
     from the sun.
15   He bestowed his spirit upon him
     so that we would preserve it for him,
     and his understanding,
     so that we would always bear him increase.

6   True God, I praise you.
     I affirm you as the beginning.
     You alone, Lord, are the beginning —
     indeed, I acknowledge no other —
5   of earth and of heaven,
     of the sea and the air
     and of all things animate and inanimate
     that are within those four.
     You alone created all of this.

10   du nebedorftest helfene dar zuo.
      ich wil dich ze anegenge haben
      in worten unt in werchen.

7   Got, du geschuofe allez daz ter ist;
      ane dih nist nieweht.
      ze aller jungest gescuofe du den man
      nah dinem bilde getan,
5   nah diner getæte,
      so su gewalt hete.
      du blise im dinen geist in,
      daz er ewich mohte sin;
      noh er nevorhte den tot,
10   ub er behielte din gebot.
      zallen eren gescuofe du den man:
      du wessest wol den sinen val.

8   Duo gescuof er ein wip,
      si waren beidiu ein lip.
      duo hiez er si wisen
      zuo dem vronem paradyse,
5   daz si da inne wæren,
      des sinen obzes phlægen;
      unt ub siu daz behielten,
      vil maneger gnaden si gewilten.
      di genade sint so mancvalt,
10   so si an den buochen stant gezalt,
      von den brunnen,
      die in paradyse springent:
      honeges rinnet Geon,
      milche rinnet Vison,
15   wines rinnet Tigris,
      oles Eufrates.
      daz scuof er den zwein ze genaden,
      di in paradyse waren.

9   Wie der man getæte,
      des gehuge wir leider note;
      dur des tiefelles rat

10   You did not require any aid in doing so.
      I will take you as my beginning
      in word and in deed.

7   God, you created everything that there is.
      Without you there is nothing.
      Last of all you created man, shaped
      according to your own image,
5   according to your form,
      as you had the power to do.
      You breathed your spirit into him
      so that he might be eternal.
      Nor would he have to fear death
10   as long as he kept your commandment.
      You created man for the highest glory.
      You were well aware that he would fall.

8   Then he created a woman.
      They were both one flesh.
      He had them led
      into blessed Paradise
5   so that they might dwell in it
      and take care of its fruit.
      And if they did so
      they would enjoy many blessings.
      The Scriptures
10   tell of the many blessings
      of the springs
      that gush forth in Paradise.
      The Gehon flows with honey.
      The Phison flows with milk.
15   The Tigris flows with wine.
      The Euphrates with oil.
      He created these things as blessings for the two people
      who dwelt in Paradise.

9   Sadly, we must needs remember
      how man acted.
      How quickly he became an exile

wi schir er ellente wart!
5   vil harte gie diu sin scult
uber alle sine afterchunft;
duo wurde wir alle gezalt
in des tiefelles gewalt.
vil michel was diu unser not:
10   duo begunde richesen der tot,
der helle wuohs der ir gewin,
manchunne allez vuor in.

10   Duo sih Adam geviel,
duo was naht unte vinster.
duo irscinen an dirre werlte
di sternen bire ziten,
5   di der vil luzzel liehtes baren
so berhte so si waren;
wante siu beschatewote
diu nebelvinster naht,
diu von dem tiefel bechom,
10   in des gewelte wir alle waren,
unze uns erscein der gotes sun,
warer sunno von den himelen.

11   Der sternen aller iegelich,
der teilet uns daz sin lieht.
sin lieht daz gab uns Abel,
daz wir durch reht ersterben.
5   duo lert unsih Enoch,
daz unsriu werch sin elliu guot.
uz der archa gab uns Noe
ze himele rehten gedingen.
duo lert unsih Abraham,
10   daz wir gote sin gehorsam,
der vil guote David,
daz wir wider ubele sin gnadich.

12   Duo irscein uns zaller jungest
Baptista Johannes,
dem morgensternen gelich:

because he listened to the Devil's counsel!
5   The great weight of his guilt
passed on to all his descendants.
That is when we were all given
into the power of the Devil.
Our misery was very great.
10   Then death began its reign.
The winnings of hell increased.
All humankind passed into it.

10   After Adam had fallen
there was darkness and night.
The stars shone on the world
at their appointed times
5   but they yielded very little light,
no matter how bright they were,
since they were overshadowed
by the dark mist of the night
that came from the Devil,
10   in whose power we all were
until the son of God appeared to us,
the true sun of the heavens.

11   Each and every one of the stars
bestows its light on us.
Abel gave us his light
so that we would die for righteousness's sake.
5   Later Enoch taught us
that all our works should be good.
From the ark Noah gave us
true hope of heaven.
Then Abraham taught us
10   to obey God.
The most excellent David,
to be merciful in the face of evil.

12   Then at last John the Baptist
shone forth for us
like the morning star.

der zeigote uns daz ware lieht,
5   der der vil wærliche was
uber alle prophetas,
der was der vrone vorbote
von dem geweltigen gote.
duo rief des boten stimme
10   in dise werltwuostunge
in spiritu Elie:
er ebenot uns den gotes wech.

13   Duo die vinf werlte
gevuoren alle zuo der helle
unte der sehsten ein vil michel teil,
duo irscein uns allen daz heil.
5   duo newas des langore bite,
der sunne gie den sternen mite;
duo irscein uns der sunne
uber allez manchunne.
in fine seculorum
10   duo irscein uns der gotes sun
in mennisclichemo bilde:
den tach braht er uns von den himelen.

14   Duo wart geborn ein chint,
des elliu disiu lant sint;
demo dienet erde unte mere
unte elliu himelisciu here,
5   den sancta Maria gebar:
des scol si iemer lop haben,
wante si was muoter unte maget
(daz wart uns sit von ir gesaget),
si was muoter ane mannes rat,
10   si bedachte wibes missetat.

15   Diu geburt was wunterlich,
demo chinde ist nieht gelich.
duo trante sih der alte strit,
der himel was ze der erde gehit.
5   duo chomen von himele

He who was truly
5   greater than all the *prophetae*
showed us the one true light.
He was the blessed messenger
of almighty God.
The voice of the messenger
10   cried into the desert of this world
in spiritu Eliae.
He made the path of God smooth for our sakes.

13   After five ages of the world
had all passed into hell
along with a great part of the sixth,
then salvation shone forth for us all.
5   Then there was no more waiting.
The sun accompanied the stars.
Then the sun shone forth for us
over all humankind.
In fine saeculorum,
10   then the son of God shone forth for us
in human form.
He brought us day from the heavens.

14   At that time a child was born
to whom all these lands belong.
The earth and the sea
and all the heavenly hosts serve him
5   whom Saint Mary bore.
She deserves to be praised forever
since she was a mother and a virgin.
We were told this about her subsequently.
She was a mother without help of any man.
10   She drew a veil over the misdeeds of woman.

15   The birth was miraculous.
There is nothing equal to the child.
That is when the ancient battle was put aside.
Earth was wed to heaven.
5   Then a great multitude of angels

der engil ein michel menige,
duo sanch daz here himelisch
'gloria in excelsis'.
wie tiure guot wille si,
10 daz sungen si sa der bi.
daz was der ereste man,
der sih in Adames sunden nie nebewal.

16 Daz chint was gotes wisheit,
sin gewalt ist michel unte breit.
duo lach der riche gotes sun
in einer vil engen chrippe.
5 der engel meldot in da,
die hirte funden in sa.
er verdolte, daz si in besniten;
duo begieng er ebreiscen site,
duo wart er circumcisus,
10 duo nanten si in Jesus.
mit opphere loste in diu maget,
des newirt von ir niht gedaget,
zwo tuben brahte si fur in:
dur unsih wolt er armer sin.

17 Antiquus dierum,
der wuhs unter den jaren;
der ie ane zit was,
unter tagen gemert er sin gewahst.
5 duo wuohs daz chint edele,
der gotes atem was in imo.
duo er drizzich jar alt was,
des disiu werlt al genas,
duo chom er zuo Jordane,
10 getoufet wart er dare.
er wuosch ab unser missetat,
nehein er selbe nine hat.
den alten namen legite wir da hine,
von der touffe wurte wir alle gotes chint.

came from heaven.
The heavenly host sang
"gloria in excelsis."
At the same time they also sang
10   about the great value of good will.
He was the first human
who had never been stained by Adam's sins.

16   The child was the wisdom of God.
His power is great and far-reaching.
Yet the mighty son of God lay
in a very small manger.
5   The angel proclaimed his presence.
The shepherds found him at once.
He allowed himself to be circumcised.
Thus he followed the Hebrew custom.
When he had been *circumcisus*
10   they named him Jesus.
It has not been kept secret that
the Virgin redeemed him with an offering.
She brought two doves for him.
For our sakes he chose to be poor.

17   *Antiquus dierum*,
he grew up subject to the passing years.
He who had always been beyond time
increased in size subject to the passing days.
5   Thus the noble child grew up.
The spirit of God was in him.
When he through whom all the world was saved
was thirty years old
he came to the Jordan.
10   He was baptized there.
He washed away our sins.
He himself has none at all.
There we put aside the old name.
Through baptism we all became children of God.

18 Sa duo nah der toufe
    diu gotheit sih ougte.
    daz was daz eriste zeichen:
    von dem wazzer machot er den win.
5   drin toten gab er den lib.
    von dem bluote nert er ein wib.
    di chrumben unt di halzen,
    di machet er alle ganze.
    den blinten er daz lieht gab,
10 neheiner mite er nephlach.
    er loste mangen behaften man,
    den tiefel hiez er dane varen.

19 Mit finf proten sat er
    vinf tusent unte mere,
    daz si alle habeten gnuoc;
    zwelf chorbe man danne truoc.
5   mit fuozzen wuot er uber fluot,
    zuo den winten chod er 'ruowet'.
    di gebunden zungen
    di lost er dem stummen.
    er ein warer gotes prunne,
10 dei heizzen vieber laschet er duo.
    diu touben oren er intsloz.
    suht von imo floh.
    den siechen hiez er uf stan,
    mit sinem bette dane gan.

20 Er was mennisch unt got.
    also suoze ist sin gebot:
    er lert uns diemuot unte site,
    triwe unte warheit dir mite,
5   daz wir uns mit triwen trageten,
    unser not ime chlageten.
    daz lert uns der gotes sun
    mit worten jouch mit werchen.
    mit uns er wantelote
10 driu unte drizzich jar,
    durch unser not daz vierde halp.

18   As soon as he had been baptized
his divinity was revealed.
This was the first sign:
he made water from wine.

5   He gave life to three dead people.
He cured a woman of the hemorrhage.
The crooked and the lame,
he made them all whole.
He gave light to the blind.

10   He required no reward.
He freed many who were possessed.
He ordered the Devil to depart.

19   With five loaves of bread he satisfied
more than five thousand
so that they all had enough.
Twelve baskets were carried away.

5   He strode across the water on his feet.
To the winds he said "be still."
He loosed
the bound tongues of the mute.
Truly a wellspring of God,

10   he quenched burning fevers.
He unlocked deaf ears.
Illness fled before him.
He called the sick to arise
and depart with their beds.

20   He was human and God.
His commandment is very gentle.
He taught us humility and proper behavior,
along with loyalty and truth,

5   so that we would bear ourselves with devotion
and pour out our misery to him.
This the son of God taught us
through words and through deeds.
He lived among us

10   thirty-three years,
on account of our need, and half of the thirty-fourth.

vil michel ist der sin gewalt.
diu siniu wort waren uns der lip.
durch unsih alle erstarb er sit:
15 er wart mit sinen willen
an daz cruce irhangen.

21 Duo habten sine hente
di veste nagelgebente,
galle unt ezzich was sin tranch:
so lost uns der heilant.
5 von siner siten floz daz pluot,
des pir wir alle geheiligot.
inzwischen zwen meintæten
hiengen si den gotes sun.
von holze huob sih der tot,
10 von holze gevil er, gote lop.
der tievel ginite an daz fleisc,
der angel was diu gotheit.
nu ist ez wol irgangen:
da an wart er gevangen.

22 Duo der unser ewart
also unsculdiger irslagen wart,
diu erda irvorht ir daz mein,
der sunne an erde ni nescein,
5 der umbehanc zesleiz sich al,
sinen herren chlagete der sal,
diu grebere taten sih uf,
di toten stuonten dar uz
mit ir herren gebote:
10 si irstuonten lebentich mit gote.
di sint unser urchunde des,
daz wir alle irsten ze jungest.

23 Er wart ein teil gesunterot
ein lucel von den engelen;
ze zeichene an dem samztage
daz fleisc ruowote in demo grabe,
5 unt an dem dritten tage

His power is very great.
His words gave us life.
Later he died for all of us.
15 He was hung on the Cross
as he himself desired.

21 His hands were held fast,
gripped by nails.
His drink was gall and vinegar.
Thus the redeemer saved us.
5 Blood flowed from his side
by which we are all sanctified.
They hung the son of God
between two malefactors.
Death arose from a tree.
10 By a tree it was defeated, praise be to God.
The Devil snatched at the flesh.
Divinity was the hook.
Things have turned out well.
He was caught on it.

22 When our high priest, though innocent,
was killed,
the crime filled the earth with fear.
The sun did not shine on the earth.
5 The curtain of the Temple fell completely to shreds.
The Temple lamented its lord.
The graves opened.
The dead arose out of them
at their lord's command.
10 They arose alive in God.
They are our proof
that we will all rise from the dead at the end.

23 Part of him was separated
for a short time from the angels.
As a sign, his body rested
in its grave on Saturday.
5 And on the third day

duo irstuont er von dem grabe.
hinnen vuor er untotlich.
after tode gab er uns den lip,
des fleisches urstente,
10   himelriche imer an ente.
nu richeset sin magenchraft
uber alle sine hantgescaft.

24   Daz was der herre, der da chom
tinctis vestibus von Bosra,
in pluotigem gewæte —
durch unsih leid er note — ,
5   vil scone in siner stole
durch sines vater ere.
vil michel was sin magenchraft
uber alle himelisc herscaft.
uber di helle ist der sin gewalt
10   michel unte manicvalt.
in bechennent elliu chunne
hie in erde joch in himele.

25   Von der Juden slahte
got mit magenchrefte
diu hellesloz er al zebrach.
duo nam er da daz sin was,
5   daz er mit sinem bluote
vil tiure chouphet hiete.
der fortis armatus
der chlagete duo daz sin hus.
duo ime der sterchore chom,
10   der zevuorte im sin geroube al;
er nam imo duo elliu sinu vaz,
der er ee so manegez hie in werlt besaz.

26   Dizze sageten uns e
di alten prophete.
duo Abel brahte daz sin lamp,
duo hiet er disses gedanc;
5   unt Abraham brahte daz sin chint,

he arose from the grave.
He went away from here immortal.
After death he gave us life,
the resurrection of the body,
10 the heavenly kingdom forever without end.
Now he reigns in majesty
over all his creation.

24 This was the lord who came
out of Bozrah *tinctis vestibus.*
In bloody garments
he had to suffer for our sakes,
5 in his stole very beautifully
for the sake of his father's glory.
He had great power
over all the heavenly host.
His power over hell is
10 great and mighty.
Every kinship acknowledges him
here on earth and in heaven.

25 After his murder by the Jews
God shattered the bonds of hell
with his great power.
Then he took what belonged to him there,
5 which he had purchased
at a great price with his blood.
Then *fortis armatus*
mourned for his domain.
When the mightier one came to him
10 he dispersed all that he had stolen.
He took all his vessels from him
who had previously possessed so many of them here in the world.

26 The prophets of old
had already told us about this.
When Abel brought his lamb
he had had this thought.
5 And when Abraham brought his child,

duo daht er her in disen sint;
unt Moyses hiez den slangen
in der wuostenunge hangen,
daz di da lachen namen,
10   di der eiterbiszic wæren.
er gehiez uns nah den wunten
an dem cruce warez lachenduom.

27   Duo got mit siner gewalt
sluoch in egyptisce lant
(mit zehen blagen er se sluoch),
Moyses der vrone bote guot,
5   er hiez slahen ein lamb.
vil tougen was der sin gedanc:
mit des lambes pluote
die ture er gesegenote,
er streich ez an daz uberture.
10   der slahente engel vuor da vure;
swa er daz pluot ane sah,
scade da inne nin gescah.

28   Daz was allez geistlich,
daz bezeichnot christinlichiu dinc.
der scate was in den hanten,
diu warheit uf gehalten.
5   duo daz mære osterlamp
chom in der Juden gewalt
unt daz opher mære
lag in crucis altare,
duo wuoste der unser wigant
10   des alten wuotriches lant.
den tievel unt allez sin here
den verswalh daz rote toufmere.

29   Von dem tode starp der tot,
diu helle wart beroubet,
duo daz mære osterlamp
fur unsih gopheret wart.
5   daz gab uns friliche widervart

he was thinking along these lines.
And Moses had the snake
hung up in the wilderness
so that those who had received poisoned bites
10 might find a cure there.
He promised us who had been wounded
true healing on the Cross.

27 When God struck the land of
Egypt with his might
(he struck them with ten plagues),
Moses, the holy messenger of God,
5 ordered a lamb to be killed.
He kept his intentions altogether secret.
He made a sign of blessing on the doors
with lamb's blood.
He smeared it on the lintel.
10 The avenging angel passed by.
Nothing was harmed inside any place
on which the angel saw blood.

28 All of this had a spiritual meaning.
It signifies that which is Christian.
The shadow was in their possession.
The truth was withheld.
5 When the blessed Easter lamb
fell into the power of the Jews
and the splendid sacrifice
lay *in crucis altari*
then our champion put to waste
10 the land of the ancient tyrant.
The Red Sea of baptism swallowed up
the Devil and all his host.

29 Death died through death.
Hell was robbed
when the splendid Easter lamb
was sacrificed for us.
5 That gave us free passage

in unser alt erbelant,
beidu wege unte lant;
dar hab wir geistlichen ganc,
daz tageliche himelprot.
10   der gotes prunno ist daz pluot:
swa daz stuont an dem uberture,
der slahente engel vuor da fure.

30   Spiritalis Israel,
nu scouwe wider din erbe,
want du irloset bist
de iugo Pharaonis.
5   der unser alte viant
der wert uns daz selbe lant,
er wil uns gerne getaren:
den wec scul wir mit wige varen.
der unser herzoge ist so guot:
10   ub uns negezwivelet daz muot —
vil michel ist der sin gewalt — ,
mit im besizze wir diu lant.

31   O crux benedicta,
aller holze besziste,
an dir wart gevangen
der gir Leviathan.
5   lip sint dine este, wante wir
den lip irnereten an dir.
ja truogen din este
di burde himelisce.
an dich floz daz frone pluot,
10   din wuocher ist suzze unte guot,
da der mite irloset ist
manchun allez daz der ist.

32   Trehtin, du uns gehieze
daz du war verlizze.
du gewerdotest uns vore sagen,
swen du, herre, wurdest irhaben
5   von der erde an daz cruce,

along roads and across territories
back into our ancient ancestral homeland.
There we move spiritually
and have the bread of heaven every day.
10   The blood is the fountainhead of God:
wherever it was on the lintel,
the avenging angel passed over.

30   *Spiritalis Israel,*
now behold your inheritance once again,
now that you have been freed
de iugo Pharaonis.
5   Our ancient enemy
wants to keep us out of that same country.
He hopes to do us harm.
We will follow that route ready to fight.
Our leader in battle is most excellent.
10   If we do not begin to doubt —
his power is very great —
we will possess those lands along with him.

31   *O crux benedicta,*
best of all trees,
the ravenous Leviathan
was caught on you.
5   Your branches are dear to us,
since our lives were saved on you.
Yea, your branches bore
the heavenly burden.
The blood of divinity flowed onto you.
10   Your fruit is sweet and good,
since all humanity that exists
is redeemed with it.

32   Lord, you have made true
what you promised us.
You deigned to prophesy to us,
Lord, that when you were lifted
5   from the earth onto the Cross,

du unsich zugest zuo ze dir.
din martere ist irvollet:
nu leste, herre, diniu wort;
nu ziuch du, chunich himelisc,
10 unser herce dar da du bist,
daz wir, dine dinestman,
von dir nesin gesceiden.

33 O crux salvatoris,
du unser segelgerte bist,
disiu werlt elliu ist daz meri,
min trehtin segel unte vere,
5   diu rehten werch unser segelseil,
diu rihtent uns di vart heim.
der segel deist der ware geloube,
der hilfet uns der zuo wole.
der heilige atem ist der wint,
10 der vuoret unsih an den rehten sint.
himelriche ist unser heimuot,
da sculen wir lenten, gote lob.

34 Unser urlose ist getan,
des lobe wir got vater al
unt loben es ouch den sinen sun
pro nobis crucifixum,
5   der dir mennisce wolte sin,
unser urteile diu ist sin.
daz dritte ist der heilige atem,
der scol uns ouch genaden.
wir gelouben daz di namen dri
10 ein wariu gotheit si.
also unsich vindet der tot,
so wirt uns gelonet.
da wir den lip namen,
dar widere scul wir. AMEN.

you would draw us up to you.
Your martyrdom has been accomplished.
Now, Lord, fulfill your words.
Now, heavenly king, draw
10   our hearts to where you are,
so that we, your servants,
will not be parted from you.

33   *O crux salvatoris*,
you are our mast.
All this world is the sea.
My Lord is sail and helmsman.
5   Good works are our sail rope.
They guide us as we travel home.
The sail is true faith.
It will help us to well-being.
The Holy Spirit is the wind
10   that guides us along the right course.
The kingdom of heaven is our home.
That is where we will land, praise be to God.

34   Our salvation has been accomplished.
For that we all praise God the father
and for the same reason praise his son as well,
pro nobis crucifixum,
5   who chose to be human.
He will judge us.
The third is the Holy Spirit,
who should have mercy on us.
We believe these three names
10   are one true Godhead.
We will be rewarded
according to the condition in which death finds us.
We will return to the place
from which we received life. Amen.

Das Annolied

Rhythmvs de S. Annone Coloniensi Archiepiscopo

1   VVir hôrten ie dikke singen
      von alten dingen:
      wî snelle helide vuhten,
      wî si veste burge brêchen,
5   wî sich liebin vuiniscefte schieden,
      wî rîche kunige al zegiengen.
      nû ist cît, daz wir dencken,
      wî wir selve sulin enden.
      Crist, der vnser héro gût,
10   wî manige ceichen her vns vure dût,
      alser ûffin Sigeberg havit gedân
      durch den diurlîchen man,
      den heiligen bischof Annen,
      durch den sînen willin.
15   dabî wir uns sulin bewarin,
      wante wir noch sulin varin
      von disime ellendin lîbe hin cin êwin,
      dâ wir îmer sulin sîn.

2   In der werilde aneginne,
      dů lîht war vnte stimma,
      dů diu vrône godis hant
      diu spêhin werch gescûph sô manigvalt,
5   dů deilti got sîni werch al in zuei:
      disi werlt ist daz eine deil,
      daz ander ist geistîn.
7a dannini lisit man, daz zuâ werilte sîn:
7b diu eine, dâ wir inne birin;
7c diu ander ist geistîn.
      dů gemengite dei wîse godis list
      von den zuein ein werch, daz der mennisch ist,

Song of Anno

A Poem about St. Anno,
Archbishop of Cologne

1   We have often heard songs
        about deeds of old:
        how valiant heroes fought,
        how they destroyed strong fortresses,
    5 how valued friendships came to an end,
        how mighty kings were completely undone.
        Now it is time for us to consider
        how we ourselves will meet our end.
        Think of the many miraculous signs
   10 that Christ, our good Lord, has placed before us,
        as he did on mount Siegberg
        for the sake of the worthy man,
        for the sake of
        the saintly bishop Anno.
   15 Therefore we should take care,
        since we will pass some day
        from this wretched life in exile into eternity,
        where we will remain forever.

2   At the beginning of the world,
        when there was light and voice,
        when the holy hand of God created
        a great multiplicity of splendid works,
    5 God divided all his works into two parts.
        This world is one part.
        The other is spiritual.
   7a Thus one reads that there are two worlds.
   7b There is one in which we exist.
   7c The other is spiritual.
        Then the wisdom and skill of God combined
        these two into a single work, the human being,

10   der beide ist, corpus unte geist;
　　　dannin ist her nâ dim engele allermeist.
　　　alle gescaft ist an dem mennischen,
　　　sôiz sagit daz evangelium.
　　　wir sulin un cir dritte werilde celin,
15　 sô wir daz die Crîchen hôrin redin.
　　　zden selben êrin ward gescaphin Adam,
　　　havit er sich behaltin.

3　　 Dû sich Lûcifer dû ce ubile gevieng,
　　　vnt Adam diu godis wort ubirgieng,
　　　dů balch sigis got desti mêr,
　　　daz her andere sîni werch sach rechte gên:
5　　 den mânen vnten sunnen,
　　　die gebin ire lîht mit wunnen;
　　　die sterrin bihaltent ire vart,
　　　si geberent vrost vnte hizze sô starc;
　　　daz fuir havit ûfwert sînin zug,
10　 dunnir unte wint irin vlug;
　　　dî wolken dragint den reginguz,
　　　nidir wendint wazzer irin vluz;
　　　mit blůmin cierint sich diu lant,
　　　mit loube dekkit sich der walt;
15　 daz wilt havit den sînin ganc,
　　　scône ist der vugilsanc.
　　　ein îwelîch ding diu é noch havit,
　　　dî emi got van êrist virgab,
　　　ne wêre die zuei gescephte,
20　 dî her gescûph die bezziste:
　　　die virkêrten sich in diu doleheit,
　　　dannin hûbin sich diu leit.

4　　 Cunt ist, wî der vîent virspûn den man,
　　　zi scalke wolter un havin.
　　　sô vůrter cir hellin
　　　die vunf werlt alle,
5　　 vnze got gesante sînin sun,
　　　der irlôste vns von den sunden.
　　　ce opfere wart her vur uns brâht,

10   which is both, *corpus* and spirit.
       For this reason humans are closest to the angels.
       All creation is contained in humankind.
       That is what the gospel says.
       We should count humans as part of the third world,
15   as we have heard the Greeks tell.
       Adam was created for this same glory,
       if he had only preserved himself.

3   When Lucifer turned to evil
       and Adam transgressed against God's word,
       God was angered all the more
       since he saw his other works following their proper courses.
5   The moon and the sun
       give their light with gladness.
       The stars keep to their paths.
       They produce cold and great heat.
       Fire draws upward.
10   Thunder and wind fly through the air.
       The clouds carry rain.
       Water directs its flow downward.
       The land adorns itself with flowers.
       The forest covers itself with leaves.
15   Wild animals have their ways of moving.
       The song of the birds is lovely.
       Each and every thing holds to the law
       that God assigned it at the beginning,
       except for the two creatures
20   that he created best of all.
       They perverted themselves and became presumptuous.
       That was the beginning of suffering.

4   It is well known how the enemy tempted man.
       He wanted to have him as his bondsman.
       Therefore he led all the five ages
       of the world to hell,
5   until God sent his son,
       who saved us from sin.
       He was brought as a sacrifice for us.

dem dôde nam her sîni maht.
ce hellin vûr her âne sunden,
10   her herite si mit gewelde.
der tiuvel virlôs den sînin gewalt,
wir wurdin al in vrîe gezalt.
in der doufe wurde wir Cristis man.
den heirrin sulin wir minnan.

5   Vp hůf Crist sînis crûcis vanin,
die zueilf bodin hîz her in diu lant varin.
vane himele gaf her un diu craft,
daz si ubirwunden diu heidinscapht.
5   Rôme ubirwant Pêtrus,
diu Criechen der wîse Paulus,
seint Andrêas in Patras,
in India der gůde Thômas,
Mathêus in Ethyôpia,
10   Symon unte Iûdas in Persia,
seinte Iacôbus in Hierusalem,
nû ist her dar in Galîcia bistén.
Iohannes dar in Epheso,
vili sůze konder predigin.
15   ûz des grabi noch wehsit himilbrôt,
daz dekkit manigirslahte nôt.
andre mertirêre manige,
sôiz wîtin ist ci sagine,
mit heiligem irin blůde
20   irvuldin Christis gemůde.
mit arbeiden quâmen si cirin heirrin,
nû havit her si mit êrin.

6   Die troiânischen Vranken,
si sulin is iemir gode danken,
daz her un sô manigin heiligin havit gesant,
sôiz dar in Koln ist gewant,
5   dâ dir restit ein sulich menige
van senti Maurîciin herige
vnt eilf tûsent megide,
durch Cristis minn irslagene,

He took away the power of death.
He went to hell without sin.
10 He warred against it with great might.
The Devil lost his power.
We were all proclaimed freemen.
Through baptism we became Christ's vassals.
We must love our lord.

5   Christ raised up the standard of his Cross.
He commanded the twelve apostles to go out into the world.
He gave them power from heaven
so that they might overcome the heathen.
5   Peter conquered Rome,
the learned Paul the Greeks,
St. Andrew in Patras,
the good Thomas in India,
Matthew in Ethiopia,
10 Simon and Judas in Persia,
St. James in Jerusalem.
Now he rests in Galicia.
In Ephesus John managed
to preach very eloquently.
15 From his grave the bread of heaven still grows,
which wards off many kinds of affliction.
Many other martyrs
carried out the will of Christ,
shedding their sacred blood,
20 as should be told everywhere.
Suffering, they approached their lord.
Now he maintains them in glory.

6   The Trojan Franks
should always thank God
for sending them the large number
of saints he sent to Cologne,
5   where a great many members of St. Maurice's army
have their resting place,
as do 11,000 virgins
killed on account of their love of Christ,

manige bischof alsô hêrin,
10   die dir ceichinhaftig wârin,
als iz mêr ist vane sent Annin.
des love wir Crist mit sange.

7   Ce Kolne was her gewîhet bischof.
des sal diu stat iemir loben got,
daz in der scônistir burge,
dî in diutischemi lande ie wurde,
5   rihtêre was der vrumigisti man,
der ie ci Rîni bequam,
ci diu daz diu stat desti hêror diuhte,
wandi si.ein sô wîse hêrdûm irlûhte,
vnte diu sîn dugint desti pertir wêri,
10   daz her einir sô hêrin stedi plêgi.
Koln ist der hêristin burge ein.
sent Anno brâht ir êre wole heim.

8   Ob ir willit bekennin
der burge aneginne,
sô virnemit vmbi die grimmin heidinscapht,
dannin den aldin burgin quam diu crapht.
5   Nînus hîz der êristi man,
dê dir ie volcwîgis bigan.
her saminôdi schilt unti sper —
des lobis was her vili ger — ,
halspergin unti brunigvn —
10   dů gart er sic cim sturm — ,
die helmi stâlîn heirti:
dû stifter heriverti.
diu liute wârin vnz an diu
vil ungeleidigete.
15   ir îwelîch haviti sîn lant,
an din andirin sich niwiht ni want.
vngewenit wârin si ci wîge.
vili lieb was daz Nîno.

9   Nînus leirti sîni man
aribeiti lîdin,

and many exalted bishops
10   who performed miracles,
as is reported about St. Anno.
For this we praise Christ with song.

7   Anno was consecrated bishop in Cologne.
The city should always praise God
that the best man
who ever came to the Rhine
5   was ruler of the most beautiful city
that was ever founded on German soil,
so that the city might appear all the more splendid
since it was illuminated by such wise rule,
and so that his excellent qualities would radiate all the more brightly
10   since he had in his care such a splendid city.
Cologne is one of the most splendid cities.
St. Anno brought it great glory.

8   If you would like to learn
about the origin of cities,
then hear about the raging heathen
from whom the ancient cities acquired their might.
5   Ninus is the name of the first man
who ever started a war.
He gathered shields and spears
(he was very eager for glory),
hauberks and shirts of mail
10   (he was arming himself for battle),
and hard steel helmets.
Then he began his military campaigns.
Until that time people had lived
without any trouble.
15   Each one had his own piece of land.
No one ever turned against the others.
They were not accustomed to warfare.
That was fine by Ninus.

9   Ninus taught his men
to endure hardship,

in gewêfinin rîtin
(daz si vreisin gidorstin irbîdin),
5   schiezin unti schirmin;
her ni lîz si nî gehirmin,
vnz er gewan ci sîner hant
elliu asiânischi lant.
dâ stiphter eine burg sint,
10   einir dageweidi wît,
drîir dageweidi lank.
michil was der sîn gewalt.
diu burg nanter nâh imo Nînivê,
dâ sint der merevisch Jônam ûzspê.

10   Sîn wîf diu hîz Semîramis.
diu alten Babilônie stiphti si
van cîgelin den alten,
die die gigandi branten,
5   dû Nimbrot der michilo
gerît un dumplîcho,
daz si widir godis vortin
einen turn worhtin
van erdin ûf ce himele.
10   des dreif si got widere,
dû her mit sînir gewalt
gedeilti si sô manigvalt
in zungin sibenzog;
sô steit iz in der werlti noch.
15   von demi gezûgi des stiphtis
worti diu Semîramis
die burchmûra viereggehtich,
vieri mîlin lank unti sescihg.
des turnis bistûnt dannoch
20   vieri dûsent lâfterin hôhc.
in der burch sint wârin
diu kuninge vili mêre.
dâ havitin ir gesez inne
Chaldêi die grimmin;
25   die heritin afder lanten,
vnzi si Hierusalem virbranten.

to ride in armor
so that they would dare to stand up to danger,
5   to throw spears, and to fence.
He never let them rest
until he had all the countries of Asia
in his power.
Later he built a city there
10   that took a day to cross in one direction,
three days in the other.
His power was great.
He called the city Nineveh, after himself.
That is where the whale later spit out Jonah.

10   His wife was called Semiramis.
She built ancient Babylon
using old tiles
that the giants had fired
5   when mighty Nimrod
foolishly proposed that they,
acting contrary to the fear of God,
should build a tower
from earth up to heaven.
10   Almighty God
prevented this
by dividing them up
into seventy different tongues.
That's the way it still is in the world today.
15   Using the materials from that edifice,
Semiramis built
the city walls in a square
sixty-four miles long.
At that time 4000 fathoms
20   of the tower still remained standing.
Afterwards the kings in the city
were very famous.
It was the seat
of the fierce Chaldeans.
25   They battled their way through many countries
until they burned Jerusalem to the ground.

11   In den cîdin iz geschach,
als der wîse Danihel gesprach,
dů her sîni tróume sagiti:
wî her gesîn havite
5   viere winde disir werilte
in dem michilin meri vehtinde,
vnz ûz dem meri giengin
vreislîchir dieri vieri.
viere winde biceichenint vier engele,
10   die plegint werilt allere;
die dier vier kunincrîche,
die diu werilt soldin al umbegrîfen.

12   Diz êristi dier was ein lewin.
si havite mennislîchin sin.
diu beceichenit vns alle kuninge,
die der wârin in Babilônia.
5   dere crapht unt ire wîsheit
gidâdun ire rîche vili breit.

13   Daz ander dier was ein beri wilde.
her havide drîvalde zeinde.
her cibrach al, daz her anequam,
vnti citrat iz vndir sînin clâwin.
5   der bizeichinôte driu kunicrîche,
diu cisamine al bigondin grîfin
dî den cîdin, dů Cîrus unti Dârîus
gewunnin chaldêischi hûs:
die zwêne rîche kuninge,
10   si cistôrtin Babilônie.

14   Das dritti dier was ein lêbarte.
vier arin vederich her havite.
der beceichinôte den criechiskin Alexanderin,
der mit vier herin vůr aftir lantin,
5   vnz her dir werilt einde
bî guldînin siulin bikante.
in India her die wůsti durchbrach,
mit zuein boumin her sich dâ gesprach.

11   At that time those things came to pass
just as wise Daniel had foretold
when he revealed that in his dreams
he had seen
5   the four winds of this world
clashing in the great sea
until four terrifying animals
went forth from the sea.
The four winds signify the four angels
10   that guard all the world.
The animals signify the four empires
that were to encompass all the world.

12   The first animal was a lioness.
It had human intelligence.
It signifies for us all the kings
that were in Babylon.
5   By their strength and their wisdom
they expanded their empires considerably.

13   The second animal was a wild bear.
It had three rows of teeth.
It tore apart whatever it encountered
and crushed it under its claws.
5   The bear signified the three kingdoms
that, together, all began to attack
at the time when Cyrus and Darius
conquered Chaldea.
These two powerful kings
10   destroyed Babylon.

14   The third animal was a leopard.
It had four eagle wings.
It signified Alexander of Greece,
who, with four armies, marched through many lands
5   until he reached the end of the world,
which he recognized by its golden columns.
In India he forced his way through the desert.
There he conferred with two trees.

    mit zuein grîfen
10 vûr her in liuften.
    in eimo glase
    liezer sich in den sê.
    dů wurfin sîn vngetrûwe man
    dié kettinnin in daz meri vram.
15 si quâdin: "obi du wollis sihen wunter,
    sô walz iémir in demo grunte!"
    dû sach her vure sich vlîzin
    manigin visc grôzin,
    half visc, half man.
20 dad diuht un uili harte vreissam.

15   Dů gedâchti der listige man,
    wî her sich mohte generian.
    der wág vûrt in in demo grunte.
    durch daz glas sach her manige wunter,
5 vnz er mit einim bluote
    daz scarphe meri gruozte.
    alsi diu vlůt des bluotis inpfant,
    si warf den heirin aniz lant.
    sô quam her widir in sîn rîche.
10 wol intfîngin un die Criechen.
    manigis wunderis genîte sich derselbe man.
    driu deil her der werilte zûme gewan.

16   Daz vierde dier ein ebir was.
    die cůnin Rômêre meindi daz.
    iz haviti îsirne clâwin —
    daz ne condi nieman gevân — ,
5 îsirni ceine vreisam:
    wî soldiz iemir werdin zam?
    wole beceichinit vns daz waltsuîn,
    daz did rîche ci Rôme sal vrî sîn.
    der ebir cîn horn trůg,
10 mit ten her sîni vîanti nidirslůg.
    her was sô michil unti vorhtsam:
    ci Rôme wart diu werlt al gehôrsam.

He flew into the air
10   with two griffins.
He had himself lowered
into the sea in a glass container.
Then his faithless men cast
the chains down into the water.
15   They said: "If you want to see marvelous things,
then roll around the ocean floor forever."
He saw many large fish
pass in front of him,
half man, half fish.
20   He found this very frightening.

15   Finally, the clever man began to wonder
how he could save his life.
The current carried him along the bottom.
He saw many marvels through the glass
5   until he irritated the rough sea
with some blood.
When the water sensed the blood,
it cast the sovereign out onto the land.
That is how he came back to his kingdom.
10   The Greeks gave him a warm welcome.
This man experienced many amazing things.
He won for himself the three parts of the world.

16   The fourth animal was a boar.
It stood for the valiant Romans.
It had iron claws.
No one could catch it.
5   It had terrible iron teeth.
How could it ever be tamed?
The wild boar signifies to us
that the Roman Empire will certainly remain free.
The boar had ten horns,
10   with which it cast down its enemies.
It was huge and fearsome.
The entire world became subject to Rome.

17   Cîn horn meintin cîn kuninge,
    dî mit Rômêrin rittint ci sturme.
    daz eilfti horn wûs vnz an den himil,
    die sterrin vuhtin imi widir.
5   iz hât ougin unti munt,
    sulich ni wart uns é kunt.
    manigi wort iz widir gode sprach,
    daz her vieli schiere gerach.
    daz biceichinit uns den Antichrist,
10   der noch in diese werlt kunftig ist,
    den got mit sînir gewelti
    cir hellin sal gesendin.
    der troúm allir sô irgîng,
    sôn der engil vane himele gischiet.

18   Rômêre scrivin cisamine
    in einir guldîne tavelin
    driuhunterit altheirrin,
    dî dir plêgin zuht unt êrin,
5   die dagis unti nahtis riedin,
    wî si ir êrin behîldin.
    den volgedin die herzogin al,
    wanti si ni woldin kuning havin.
    dů santin si den edelin Cêsarem,
10   dannin noch hiude kuninge heizzint keisere.
    si gâvin imi manige scar in hant,
    si hiezin un vehtin wider diutsche lant.
    dâ aribeiti Cêsar (daz ist wâr)
    mêr dan cîn ihâr,
15   sô her die meinstreinge man
    niconde nie biduingan.
    ci iungist gewan hers al ci gedinge.
    daz soltin cin êrin brengin.

19   Vndir bergin ingegin Suâben
    hîz her vanin ûf haben,
    deri vordirin wîlin mit herin
    dari cumin wârin ubir meri.
5   mit mislîchemo volke

17 The ten horns stood for the ten kings
 who rode into battle with the Romans.
 The eleventh horn grew up to heaven.
 The stars fought against it.
5 It had eyes and a mouth,
 something we had never heard of before.
 It uttered many words against God.
 For this he took quick vengeance.
 It signifies for us the Antichrist,
10 who is still to come into this world,
 whom almighty God
 will cast into hell.
 The entire dream came to pass
 as the heavenly angel had indicated.

18 On a tablet of gold
 the Romans inscribed
 the names of 300 senators,
 who maintained order and respect
5 and who discussed day and night
 how they might preserve their preeminence.
 All the leaders followed them,
 since they did not want to have a king.
 That was when they sent out noble Caesar,
10 after whom kings are called *Kaiser* even today.
 They placed many troops under his command.
 They ordered him to fight against the German lands.
 In truth, Caesar struggled
 more than ten years
15 without being able to overcome
 those mighty men.
 In the end he won them over to a treaty.
 That was to bring him to glory.

19 At the foot of the mountains
 he ordered his standards raised against the Swabians,
 whose forebears had arrived there
 long ago in large numbers from across the sea.
5 With a disparate group of people

si slûgen iri gecelte
ane dem berge Suêvo,
dannin wurdin si geheizin Suâbo:
ein liut ci râdi vollin gût,
10   redispêh genûg,
die sich dikke des vure nâmin,
daz si gûde rekkin wêrin,
woli vertig vnti wîchaft.
doch bedwang Cêsar al iri craft.

20   Dû sich Beirelant wider in virmaz,
die mêrin Reginsburch, her se bisaz.
dâ vanter inne
helm unti brunigen,
5   manigin helit gûdin,
die dere burg hûdin.
wiliche knechti dir wêrin,
deist in heidnischin bûchin mêri.
dâ lisit man: 'Noricus ensis',
10   daz diudit 'ein suert beierisch',
wanti si woldin wizzen,
daz ingeini baz nibizzin,
die man dikke durch den helm slûg.
demo liute was ie diz ellen gût.
15   dere geslehte dare quam wîlin êre
von Armenie der hêrin,
dâ Nôê ûz der arkin gîng,
dûr diz olizuî von der tûvin intfieng.
iri ceichin noch du archa havit
20   ûf den bergin Ararat.
man sagit, daz dar in halvin noch sîn,
die dir diutischin sprecchin,
ingegin India vili verro.
Peiere vûrin ie ci wîge gerno.
25   den sigin, den Cêsar an un gewan,
mit bluote mûster in geltan.

21   Der Sahsin wankeli mût
dedimo leidis genûg:

they had pitched their tents
at Mt. Suevo.
That is why they were called Swabians.
They are a people very good at council
10   and quite eloquent,
who frequently distinguished themselves
as excellent fighters,
always ready and warlike.
Nevertheless, Caesar overcame their entire fighting strength.

20   When Bavaria presumed to oppose him
he besieged the splendid city of Regensburg.
Within the city he found
helmets and shirts of mail
5   and many excellent heroes
who were guarding the city.
The books of the ancients tell
what sort of fighters they were.
In these books one can read about *Noricus ensis*,
10   which means "a Bavarian sword,"
since they were convinced
that there were none that cut better.
They often cut through helmets with them.
This people had always profited from bravery.
15   Their tribe had arrived long ago
from the highlands of Armenia,
where Noah went forth from the ark
after he had received the olive branch from the dove.
There are still signs of the ark
20   on the mountains of Ararat.
It is said that there are still people
who speak German there,
very far off in the direction of India.
The Bavarians were always eager to go to war.
25   Caesar had to pay in blood
for his victory over them.

21   The fickleness of the Saxons
caused him plenty of trouble.

sôr si wând al ubirwundin havin,
sô wârin simi aver widiri.

5 die lisit man daz si wîlin wêrin al
des wunterlîchin Alexandris man,
der diu werlt in iârin zuelevin
irvúr uns an did einti.
dů her ci Babilônie sîn einti genam,

10 dů cideiltin diz rîchi viere sîni man,
dî dir al dů woltin kuninge sîn.
dandere vůrin irre,
vnz ir ein deil mit scifmenigin
quâmin nidir cir Eilbin,

15 dâ die Duringe dů sâzin,
die sich wider un vermâzin.
cin Duringin dů dir siddi was,
daz si mihhili mezzir hiezin sahs,
der dî rekkin manigis drůgin.

20 dâmidi si die Duringe slûgin
mit untrûwin ceiner sprâchin,
die ci vridin si gelobit havitin.
von den mezzerin alsô wahsin
wurdin si geheizzin Sahsin.

25 svie si doch ire ding ane vîngen,
si můstin Rômêrin alle dienin.

22 Cêsar bigonde nâhin
zů den sînin altin mâgin,
cen Franken din edilin;
iri beidere vorderin

5 quâmin von Troie der altin,
dů die Criechin diu burch civaltin,
dů ubir diu heri beide
got sîn urteil sô irsceinte,
daz die Troiêri sum intrunnin,

10 die Criechin ni gitorstin heim vindin:
want in den cîn iârin,
dů si ci dere sâzin wârin,
sô gehîetin heimi al iri wîf,
si rieten an iri manni lîf.

When he thought he had overcome them
they turned against him again.
5   You can read that they were all at one time
followers of the amazing Alexander,
who reached the very end of the world
in twelve years.
When he met his end in Babylon
10   his empire was divided up
by four of his men, who now wanted to be kings.
The rest wandered far and wide,
until one group
came to the Elbe in a fleet of ships.
15   This place had already been settled by the Thuringians,
who made bold to resist them.
Among the Thuringians it was the custom
to call long knives *sahs*.
The fugitive warriors carried many of these knives.
20   At a meeting that had been agreed on to make peace
they broke their word
and slew the Thuringians.
They were called Saxons
on account of these very sharp knives.
25   No matter how they started out,
all of them had to serve the Romans.

22   Caesar approached
the noble Franks,
who were related to him from long ago.
Their forebears on both sides
5   had left the ancient city of Troy
when it was leveled by the Greeks,
when God revealed his judgment
on the two armies by allowing
some of the Trojans to escape.
10   The Greeks, however, did not dare to return home,
since during the ten years
they laid siege to Troy
their wives back home had all married.
They were planning to take their husbands' lives.

15   des ward irslagin der kuning Agamemno.
      irri vûrin dandero,
      vns Vlix gesindin
      der ciclôps vraz in Sicilia,
      das Vlixes mit spiezin wol gerach,
20   dúr slâfinde imi sîn ouge ûzstach.
      das geslehte deri ciclôpin
      was dannoch in Siciliin,
      alsô hó sô cîmpoume;
      an dem eindo hatten si ein ouge.
25   nû havit si got van vns virtribin hinnan
      in daz gewelde hinehalf India.

23   Troiêri vûrin in der werilte
      wîdin irri after sedele,
      vns Elenus, ein virherit man,
      des kûnin Ektoris witiwin genam,
5   mit ter er dâ ce Criechin
      bisaz sînir vîanti rîche.
      si worhtin dar eini Troie,
      dî man lange sint mohte scowen.
      Antenor was gevarn dannin ér,
10   dûr irchôs, daz Troie solti cigên.
      der stifted vns diu burg Pitavium
      bî demi wazzere Timavio.
      Enêas irvaht im Walilant.
      dâr diu sú mit trîzig iungin vant,
15   dâ worhten si diu burg Albâne,
      dannin wart sint gestiftit Rôma.
      Franko gesaz mit den sîni
      vili verre nidir bî Rîni.
      dâ worhtin si dů mit vrowedin
20   eini luzzele Troie.
      den bach hîzin si Sante
      nâ demi wazzere in iri lante;
      den Rîn havitin si vure diz meri.
      dannin wûhsin sint vreinkischi heri.
25   dî wurden Cêsari al unterdân,
      si wârin imi îdoch sorchsam.

15 That is why King Agamemnon was killed.
The others traveled around aimlessly,
until in Sicily the cyclops
devoured the retinue of Ulysses,
which Ulysses avenged by poking the cyclops's eye out
20 with a spear while he was sleeping.
The race of the cyclops,
which lived at that time in Sicily,
was as tall as the cypress trees.
They had one eye in their forehead.
25 Now God has driven them away from us
into the forests on the other side of India.

23 The Trojans wandered about the world
far and wide looking for a place to settle
until Helenus, who had been defeated,
married the widow of brave Hector,
5 with whom he took possession
of his enemies' kingdom in Greece.
There they built a Troy
that could still be seen a long time afterwards.
Antenor had left earlier
10 when he realized that Troy would perish.
He founded the city of Padua
on the river Timavus.
Aeneas won Italy for himself by force.
There where he found the sow with thirty piglets
15 they built the city of Alba,
from which Rome was later established.
Franko settled with his followers
far away on the Rhine.
There they were happy to build
20 a little Troy.
They named the brook Sante
after the river in their country.
They took the Rhine in the place of the sea.
From that time on, the Frankish people increased there.
25 They all became subject to Caesar.
However, they caused him much trouble.

24 Dů Cêsar dů widere ci Rôme gesan,
   si ni woltin sîn niht intfân.
   si quâdin, daz her durch sîni geile
   haviti virlorin des heris ein michil deil,
 5 daz her in vremidimo lante
   ân urlof sô lange havite.
   mit zorne her dů widir wante
   ci diutischimo lante,
   dâ her hât irkunnit
 10 manigin helit vili gût.
   her sante zû den heirrin,
   die dar in rîche wârin.
   her clagitin allin sîni nôt,
   her bôt un golt vili rôt.
 15 her quad, daz her si wolti gern irgezzin,
   obir un ieht ce leide gedân hetti.

25 Dů si virnâmin sînin wille,
   si saminôtin sich dar alle:
   v̂zir Gallia unti Germânia
   quâmin imi scarin manige,
 5 mit schînintin helmen,
   mit vestin halspergin.
   si brâhtin manigin scônin schiltrant.
   als ein vlût vûrin sin daz lant.
   dů ci Rôme her bigondi nâhin,
 10 dů irvorhtini dar manig man,
   wanti si sâgin schînin
   sô breite scarin sîni
   vanin ingegin burtin;
   des lîbis si alle vorhtin.
 15 Câto unti Pompêius
   rûmiti rômischi hûs;
   al der senâtus,
   mit sorgen vluhin si diurûz.
   her vûr un náh iaginta,
 20 wîtini slahinta
   vnz in Egypti lant.
   sô michil ward der herebrant.

24   When Caesar headed back to Rome
      the Romans did not want to receive him.
      They claimed that a large part of the army had been lost
      through his presumption
5   because he had stayed in foreign lands
      for such a long time without permission.
      In anger he returned
      to German lands,
      where he had gotten to know
10   many very brave warriors.
      He sent messages to the leaders
      who ruled there.
      He lamented his trouble to all of them.
      He offered them bright red gold.
15   He said he wanted to make good
      any harm he might have done them.

25   When they heard what he had in mind
      they all assembled in one place.
      Many troops came to him
      from Gallia and Germania
5   with shining helmets
      and strong coats of mail.
      They brought many excellent shields.
      They streamed into the country like a flood.
      As Caesar came closer and closer to Rome
10   and the inhabitants saw
      such a vast army glistening in the sun,
      bearing his standards against them,
      many were seized by fear.
      All were afraid for their lives.
15   Cato and Pompey
      left their Roman home.
      The entire Senate
      fled the city in fear.
      Caesar pursued them,
20   hunting them down everywhere
      as far as Egypt.
      Mighty was the fire of war.

26   VVer móhte gecelin al die menige,
     die Cêsari îltin ingeginne
     van ôstrit allinthalbin,
     alsi der snê vellit ûffin alvin,
  5 mit scarin unti mit volkin,
     alsi der hagil verit van den wolkin!
     mit minnerigem herige
     genanter an die menige.
     dů ward diz hêristi volcwîg,
  10 alsô diz bůch quît,
     daz in disim merigarten
     ie geurumit wurde.

27   Oy wî dî wîfini clungin,
     dâ dî marih cisamine sprungin!
     herehorn duzzin,
     becche blůtis vluzzin,
  5 derde diruntini diuniti,
     dî helli ingegine gliunte,
     dâ dî hêristin in der werilte
     sůhtin sich mit suertin.
     dů gelach dir manig breiti scari
  10 mit blůte birunnin gari.
     dâ mohte man sîn douwen,
     durch helme virhouwin,
     des rîchin Pompêiis man.
     dâ Cêsar den sige nam.

28   Dů vrouwite sich der iunge man,
     daz her die rîche al gewan.
     Her vûr dů mit gewelte
     ci Rôme suî sô her wolte.
  5 Rômêre, dů sin infiengin,
     einin nûwin sidde aneviengin:
     si begondin igizin den heirrin.
     daz vundin simi cêrin,
     wanter eini dů habite allin gewalt,
  10 der é gideilit was in manigvalt.
     den sidde hîz er dů cêrin

26 Who could count the multitudes
  who hastened towards Caesar
  from everywhere in the East,
  as the snow falls on the Alps,
5 armies and people,
  as the hail falls from the clouds!
  He dared to oppose these great numbers
  with the smaller army.
  Books tell us
10 that this was the mightiest battle
  that two armies ever waged
  against each other in this world.

27 Alas, how the armor resounded
  wherever the war horses charged together!
  Battle trumpets filled the air.
  Blood flowed in streams.
5 The earth thundered beneath them.
  Hell cast its glow upon the place
  where the mightiest in the world
  pursued each other with swords.
  A vast expanse of troops lay there
10 drenched completely with blood.
  There the men of mighty Pompey could be seen,
  struck through their helmets,
  dying
  where Caesar won the victory.

28 The young man rejoiced then,
  since he had conquered every kingdom.
  Next he marched to Rome with a mighty force,
  just as he wished.
5 When the Romans received him
  they instituted a new custom.
  They began to address their ruler with *ihr*.
  They thought this up to honor him,
  since he alone held all the power
10 that previously had been divided up among many.
  He had this custom taught

diutischi liuti lêrin.
ce Rôme deddir ûf daz scazhûs,
manig cieri nam her dan ûz,

15   her gébite sînin holdin
mit pellin ioch mit golte.
sidir wârin diutschi man
ce Rôme lîf unti wertsam.

29   Dů Cêsar sîn einti genam,
vnte der sîn neve gůt diu rîchi gewan,
Augustus der mêre man —
Owisburg ist nâ imi geheizan;

5   diu stifte ein sîn stîfsun,
Drûsus genanter — ,
dů ward gesant heirro Agrippa,
daz her diu lant birehta,
daz her eini burg worhte,

10   ci diu daz in dad liut vorte.
diu burg hîz her Colônia,
dâ wârin sint hêrrin maniga;
avir nâ selbe demo namin sînin
ist si geheizin Agrippîna.

30   Ci dere burg vili dikki quâmin
dî waltpodin vane Rôme,
dî dir oug êr dar in lantin
veste burge havitin:

5   Wurmiz unti Spîri,
die si worhtin al die wîli,
dů Cêsar dar in lante was
vnter die Vrankin unter saz.
dů worhter dâ bî Rîne

10   sedilhove sîne.
Meginza was dû ein kastel,
iz gemêrte manig helit snel;
dâ ist nû dere kuninge wîchtûm,
dis pâbis senitstûl.

15   Mezze stifte ein Cêsaris man,
Mezius geheizan.

to the Germans as an honor.
In Rome he opened up the treasury.
He took out large quantities of jewelry.
15   He gave gold and precious silks
to those who had been loyal to him.
From that time on, German men
were popular and esteemed in Rome.

29   When Caesar met his end
and the empire was taken over by his noble nephew,
the celebrated Augustus —
Augsburg is named after him;
5   it was founded by one of his stepsons
named Drusus —
prince Agrippa was dispatched
to establish order in the provinces
and to build a city
10   so that the people would fear him.
He named the city Cologne.
It has had many rulers since then.
In addition it is called Agrippina
after his own name.

30   Frequently commissioners would come
to this city from Rome,
who already possessed fortified cities
in the country:
5   Worms and Speyer,
which they had built
when Caesar was in the country
gaining a foothold among the Franks.
That was when he built his residences
10   along the Rhine.
At that time Mainz was a fortified place.
It was enlarged by many an intrepid hero.
Now it is the place where kings are consecrated
and the seat of papal synods.
15   One of Caesar's men, named Metius,
founded Metz.

Triere was ein burg alt —
si cierti Rômêre gewalt — ,
dannin man unter dir erdin
20   den wîn santi verri
mit steinîn rinnin
den hêrrin al ci minnin,
die ci Kolne wârin sedilhaft:
vili michil was diu iri craft.

31   In des Augusti cîtin gescahc,
daz got vane himele nider gesach.
dů ward giborin ein kuning,
demi dienit himilschi dugint:
5   Iêsus Christus, godis sun,
von der megide sente Mâriun.
des erschinin sân ci Rôme
godis zeichin vrône:
v̂zir erdin diz lûter olei spranc,
10   scône ranniz ubir lant;
vmbe diu sunnin ein creiz stûnt,
alsô rôt sô viur unti blût.
wanti dů bigondi nâhin,
dannin uns allin quam diu genâde:
15   ein niuwe kunincrîchi.
demi můz diu werilt al intwîchin.

32   Senti Pêtir, dir boto vrône,
den diuvil ubirwantir ce Rôme.
her rehte dâ ûf dis heiligin crûcis ceichin,
her screif diu burg ci Cristis eigine.
5   dannin santir drî heilige man,
ci predigene den Vrankan:
Eucharium unti Valêrium,
der dritti geinti ûffin leige.
dâ kêrdin dî zvêne widere,
10   senti Pêtri daz ce clagine.
dari santer dů sînin staf,
den legitin si ûffe Maternis graf.
si hîzin un wider von dem tôd erstân,

Trier was an old city.
The mighty Romans embellished it.
From Trier wine was sent in stone conduits
20   a long way
under ground
out of devotion to the lords
who resided in Cologne.
Their power was very great.

31   It came to pass in the time of Augustus
that God looked down from heaven.
Then a king was born
who is served by the heavenly hosts,
5   Jesus Christ, son of God,
born of St. Mary the Virgin.
That was why the sacred signs of God
appeared in Rome just then.
Pure oil gushed forth from the earth
10   and ran copiously over the land.
A circle surrounded the sun
as red as fire and blood.
For this was the dawn
of that which brought salvation to us all:
15   a new kingdom
for which all the world must make way.

32   The blessed apostle St. Peter
vanquished the Devil in Rome.
There he set up the sign of the blessed Cross.
He made the city over to Christ.
5   From there he dispatched three holy men
to preach to the Franks:
Eucharius and Valerius;
the third met his end on a cliff.
The other two returned to St. Peter
10   to lament this development.
St. Peter sent his staff,
which they placed on Maternus's grave.
They commanded him to rise from death

in senti Pêtiris gibote mit un ce Vrankin gân.
15 dů her sînis meisteris namin virnam,
her ward un sân gihôrsam.
dů intloich sich diu molta,
als iz got wolta.
her vieng sich ci demi grasi,
20 schiere îlter ûs demo gravi,
dâr vîrcig dagi hatti gilegin;
dů mûster vîrcig iâr lebin.
cêrist si dû ci Trierin lêrtin,
darná si Kolni bikêrtin,
25 dâ bischof ward derselbe man,
der vane demi tôdi was irstantan.

33   Dů gewunnin si dâ ci Vrankin
ci godis dienisti vili manigin man
mit beizzirimo wîge,
dan si Cêsar gewanne wîlen.
5   si lêrtin si widir sunde vehtin,
daz si ci godi wêrin gůde knechte.
dere lêre sint wole plâgin,
dî bischove nâh in wârin,
drî unti drîzig gezalt
10 vns ane seint Annin gewalt.
dere sint nû heilig sibine;
die schînint uns von himele,
als iz sibin sterrin nahtis dûnt.
seint Anno, lieht is her unti gůt:
15 vntir dandere brâhter sînin schîm
alsi der jachant in diz guldîni vingerlîn.

34   Den vili tiurlîchin man
muge wir nû ci bîspili havin,
den als ein spiegil anesîn,
die tugint unti wârheiti wollen plegin.
5   dů der dritte keiser Heinrîch
demi selbin heirrin bival sich,
vnti der godis willo was irgangin,
dar her ci Kolne ward mit lobe intfangin,

and to accompany them to Franconia as St. Peter had ordained.
15   When he heard the name of his master
he obeyed them at once.
Thereupon the earth opened up
as God willed it.
He held on to the grass.
20   He hurried quickly out of the grave
in which he had lain for forty days.
He still had to live another forty years.
At first they taught in Trier.
Then they converted Cologne,
25   where the same man became bishop
who had risen from the dead.

33   In Franconia they won many men
for the service of God,
in a better fight
than the one in which Caesar had won them previously.
5   They taught them to fight against sin
so that they would be good soldiers of God.
Later this teaching was spread
by the bishops who followed them,
who number thirty-three
10   up to the reign of St. Anno.
Of these, seven are now saints.
They shine down on us from heaven
like the seven stars at night.
St. Anno is radiant and splendid.
15   He added his brilliance to the others
as the hyacinth adds its brilliance to a golden ring.

34   Now we can take this most worthy man
as an example,
to be regarded as a model
by those who want to cultivate excellence and truth.
5   After Emperor Henry III
had placed his trust in this lord
and God's will had been accomplished,
Anno entered Cologne with a multitude of people

dů gieng her mit liut crefte:
10 alsi diu sunni dût in den liufte,
diu inzuschin erden unti himili geit,
beiden halbin schînit,
alsô gieng der bischof Anno
vure gode unti vure mannen.
15 in der phelinzin sîn tugint sulich was,
daz un daz rîch al untersaz,
ci godis diensti in den gebérin,
samir ein engil wêri.
sîn êre gihîlter wole beidinthalb.
20 dannin ward her ci rehtimi hêrtûmi gezalt.

35 Sîn gůte bikanti vil unmanig man.
nû virnemit, wî sîni siddi wârin gedân:
offen was her sînir worte,
vure dir wârheite niemannin her ni vorte.
5 als ein lewo saz her vur din vuristin,
als ein lamb gîn her untir diurftigin.
den tumbin was her sceirphe,
den gůtin was er einste.
weisin unti widewin,
10 die lobitin wole sînin sidde.
sîni predigi unti sîn ablâz
nimohti nichein bischof důn baz,
alsô gotlîche,
dad iz mit rehte solte lîchen
15 allir irdischir diet.
gode was her vili liep.
sêliclîche stûnt kolnischi werlt,
dů si sulichis bischovis wârin wert.

36 Sô diz liut nahtis ward slâfin al,
sô stûnt imi ûf der vili gůte man.
mit lûterer sînir venie
sûhter munistere manige.
5 sîn oblei her mit imi drůg,
dir armin vant her genúg,
die dir selide niht hattin

and was welcomed with jubilation.
10   As the sun moving through the air
passes between heaven and earth
and shines in both directions,
so Bishop Anno passed
before God and humans.
15   At the palace his power was so great
that all the imperial princes sat below him.
In the service of God he carried himself
as if he were an angel.
He preserved his good name in both camps.
20   Therefore he was counted among the true rulers.

35   Very few people recognized his goodness.
Now hear how he lived and acted.
He was open in his speech.
He feared no one on account of the truth.
5   He sat before the princes like a lion.
He went among the poor like a lamb.
Towards the foolish he was strict.
Towards the virtuous he was benevolent.
Orphans and widows praised him
10   highly for the way he acted.
He could give sermons and indulgences
better than any other bishop,
in such a holy manner
that all people on earth
15   should rightly have approved.
He was beloved of God.
The people of Cologne were blessed by good fortune
when they were worthy of such a bishop.

36   At night, when all the people were sleeping,
this most holy man roused himself.
He sought out many of the monastery churches,
where he would kneel, pure in heart, and say his prayers.
5   He carried with him the offerings he had received.
He found plenty of poor people
who had no roofs over their heads

vnt imi dâ ware dâdin.
dâ diz armi wîf mit demi kindi lag,
10   der dir nieman ni plag,
dari gienc der bischof vrôno;
her gebettidi iri selbe scôno,
sô her mit rehte mohte heizin
vatir aller weisin.
15   sô harte was er in genêdig.
nû havitis imi got gelônit.

37   Vili sêliclîche diz rîche alliz stûnt,
dů dis girihtis plag der heirre gůt,
dů her zô ci demi rîchi
den iungen Heinrîche.
5   wilich rihtêre her wêre,
das quam wîtini mêre.
van Criechin unt Engelantin
die kuninge imi gebi santin;
sô dedde man von Denemarkin,
10   von Vlanterin unti Riuzilanti.
manig eigin her ci Kolni gewan.
dî munister cierter ubir al.
ci demi tiurin gotis lobe stiftir
selbo vier munister;
15   diz vunfti ist Sigeberg, sîn vili liebi stat,
dar ûffe steit nû sîn graf.

38   Ni avir diu michil êre
iewiht wurre sînir sêlin,
sô dede imi got, alsô dir goltsmit důt,
sôr wirkin willit eine nuschin gůt:
5   diz golt siudit her in eimi viure;
mit wêhim werki důt her si tiure,
mit wierin alsô cleinin;
wole slîft her die goltsteine;
mit manigir slahtin gigerwa
10   gewinnit er in die variwa.
alsô sleif got seint Annin
mit arbeidin manigin.

and who were watching for him.
The blessed bishop went
10   to where a woman lay with her child
without anyone at all to care for her.
He prepared her bed himself with care
so that he can rightly be called
the father of all orphans,
15   he showed them so much mercy.
Now God has rewarded him for this.

37   The entire empire enjoyed good fortune
when this excellent lord held power,
when he was raising young Henry
to rule.
5   Reports about the sort of regent he was
spread far and wide.
The kings of Greece and England
sent him gifts,
as they did from Denmark,
10   from Flanders and Russia.
He acquired much property in Cologne.
He decorated churches everywhere.
He himself founded four monasteries
to the precious glory of God.
15   The fifth is Siegberg, a place that was especially dear to him,
where his grave now lies.

38   In order to keep his great fame
from harming his soul in any way
God acted towards him as a goldsmith acts
when he wants to fashion a fine brooch.
5   He melts the gold over a fire.
His skillful craftsmanship
increases the value of the brooch with fine gold wires.
He polishes the topazes smooth.
He brings out their color
10   with all sorts of preparations.
Thus God polished St. Anno
with many sorts of travail.

39   Dikki un anevuhtin dî lantheirrin,
     ci iungis brâht iz got al ci sînin êrin.
     vili dikki un anerietin,
     dî une soltin bihûtin.
5   wî dikki une dî virmanitin,
     dî her ci heirrin brâht havite!
     ci iungis niwart daz niht virmidin,
     her niwurde mit gewêfinin ûze dir burg virtribin,
     also Absalon wîlin
10   virtreib vater sînin,
     den vili gûtin David.
     disi zuei dinc, harti si wârin gelîch.
     leidis unte arbeite genúg
     genîte sich der heirro gût,
15   al náh dis heiligin Cristis bilide.
     dů súnt iz got van himele.

40   Dar nâh vîng sich ane der ubile strît,
     des manig man virlôs den lîph,
     dů demi vierden Heinrîche
     virworrin wart diz rîche.
5   mort, roub unti brant
     civûrtin kirichin unti lant
     von Tenemarc unz in Apuliam,
     van Kerlingin unz an Ungerin.
     den nîman nimohte widir stén,
10   obi si woltin mit trûwin unsamit gên,
     die stiftin heriverte grôze
     wider nevin unti hûsgenôze.
     diz rîche alliz bikêrte sîn gewêfine
     in sîn eigin inâdere.
15   mit siginuftlîcher ceswe
     vbirwant iz sich selbe,
     daz dî gidouftin lîchamin
     vmbigravin ciworfin lâgin
     ci âse den bellindin,
20   den grâwin walthundin.
     dů daz ni trúite bisûnin seint Anno,
     dů bidrôz une lebin langere.

39   The lords of the realm attacked him frequently.
God turned everything to Anno's own glory in the end.
Those who were supposed to protect him
often planned attacks on him.
5   How often he was scorned
by those whom he had brought to power!
In the end he was not even spared this:
he was driven out of the city by force of arms,
just as Absalom
10   drove out his father,
the godly David, long ago.
These two events were very similar.
The noble prince had to endure
much hardship and suffering,
15   entirely according to the example of the blessed Christ.
God in heaven repaid him for this.

40   After this the wretched struggle began
in which many lost their lives,
when the empire was brought into confusion
against Henry IV.
5   Murder, robbery, and arson
devastated the churches and the countryside
from Denmark into Apulia,
from France as far as Hungary.
The very ones who would have been unconquerable
10   if they had acted together in good faith
undertook great military campaigns
against their relatives and countrymen.
The whole empire turned its weapons
against its own entrails.
15   With its own victorious right hand
it conquered itself,
so that Christian corpses
lay strewn about unburied,
as carrion for the howling
20   gray wolves.
When St. Anno no longer believed in the possibility of reconciliation
he found it a burden to live any longer.

41   Her reit ci Salivelt in Duringe lant.
        dâ irbaritimi got diu sîni hant:
        einis dagis ingegin nône
        dir himil indedde sich scône;
5   dâ sach her inne
        diu gotelîche wunne,
        dî her nidorsti kundin
        nicheinimo weriltlîchim manne.
        dů her ûffe sînim wagene lag,
10   vnter sînis gebeddis plag,
        sulich mâncraft un umbevieng,
        daz man sescein ros ci demo wagine spien.
        dů dûht hun, daz her sêge,
        suad sôdor iemir kunftig wêre.
15   vili harte untirquam sigis der heilige man;
        dů bigondir dannin sîchen.

42   Einis nahtis der heirro dů gesach,
        wî her quam in einin vili kuniglîchin sal
        ci wuntirlîchimi gesidele,
        sô iz mit rehti solde sîn ci himele.
5   dů dûht un in sînim troume,
        wîz allinthalvin wêre bihangin mit golde.
        dî viuli tiurin steini liuhtin dar ubiral,
        sanc unti wunne was dir grôz unti manigvalt.
        dů sâzin dar bischove manige,
10   si schinin alsô die sterrin cisamine.
        dir bischof Bardo was ir ein,
        senti Heribret gleiz dar als ein goltstein.
        andere heirin genúg:
        vn was ein lebin unt ein mût.
15   dů stûnt dir ein stûl ledig unt eirlîch;
        seint Anno wart sînis vili gemeit.
        her was ci sînin êrin dar gesat;
        nû lobit hers got, dad iz alsô gescach.
        ô wî gerne her dů gesêze,
20   den lîbin stûl wî gerner bigriffe!
        dad ni woltin gelôbin dî vurstin
        durch einin vlekke vure sînin brustin.

41   He rode to Saalfeld in the land of the Thuringians.
       There God revealed his power to him.
       One day around noon
       the sky opened up in splendor.
  5 Within he beheld
       the glory of God,
       something which he did not dare reveal
       to anybody in this world.
       When he lay in his wagon
 10 and said his prayers,
       such a force came over him
       that sixteen horses had to be harnessed to the wagon.
       He thought he was seeing
       everything that would happen in the future.
 15 The holy man was very much afraid.
       Then he became sick.

42   One night the prince saw
       himself enter a very majestic hall
       containing marvelous thrones,
       just like those that are quite rightly supposed to be in heaven.
  5 It seemed to him in his dream
       as if the hall had been hung throughout with cloth of gold.
       The most precious gems shone everywhere.
       He heard singing there and jubilation, great and various.
       Many bishops were seated there.
 10 They shone together like the stars.
       Bishop Bardo was one of them.
       St. Heribert glistened like a topaz.
       Many other princes of the church were there.
       They shared a single way of living and a single way of thinking.
 15 One of the thrones there stood empty and magnificent.
       St. Anno was very glad to see that.
       It had been placed there in his honor.
       He praised God that things had turned out that way.
       Oh, how he would have liked to sit there!
 20 How he would have liked to take possession of that precious throne!
       The princes would not allow that
       because of a spot on his chest.

43 Vf stûnt dir heirrin ein, hîz Arnolt;
  ci Wurmizi was her wîlin bischof.
  seint Annin nam her mit handin,
  sô quâmin si dar bihalvin.
5 mit sûzir redin her un dû bistûnt.
  her sprach: "trôsti dig, heirro, godis drût!
  disin vlekkin wîsi hine gedûn!
  ci wâre, dir is gereit der êwigi stûl.
  daz sal sîn in curtin stundin,
10 sô bistu disin heirrin willicumin.
  vntir un nimaht tu nû blîvin.
  wî lûtir iz sal sîn, dad si willin lîdin!
  Crist havit tir disi ding irougit.
  ô wî, heirro, wad tir êrin unti genâdin volgit!"
15 harti gînc iz imi ci hercin,
  daz her widere kêrin solde zir erdin.
  ni wêrit dû ci stundin sô gewant,
  durch alle diusi werilt ni rúmiter daz paradysi lant:
  sulich is diu himilschi wunne.
20 dar sule wir denkin, alt unti iungin.
  von demi slâfe dir heirro dû gestûnt,
  wole wister, wad her solde dûn:
  Kolnêrin virgab her sîni hulte.
  daz her si hazzite, wî grôz daz wârin ere sculte!

44 Dû dat cît dû bigonde nâhen,
  daz imi got wolte lônin,
  dû ward her gikeistigit
  alsi dir heiligi Iôb wîlin:
5 vane vûzin vns an diz hoibit
  sô harti al bitoibit.
  sô schît diu tiure sêla
  von mennislîchimo sêra,
  von disimo siechin lîbi
10 in das êwigi paradysi.
  diz vleisc intfînc du erda,
  dir geist vûr up ci berga.
  dari sule wir iemir nâh imo deinkin,
  wâ wir ci iungist sulin leintin.

43   One of the princes, called Arnold, stood up.
He had been bishop of Worms.
He took St. Anno by the hand
so that they approached the place side by side.
5   He addressed him kindly.
He said: "Be comforted, sir, beloved of God.
Arrange for this blemish to be removed.
Truly, this eternal throne is prepared for you.
It will come to pass very soon
10   that these lords will welcome you.
You may not remain among them now.
For them to put up with something, it must be very pure indeed.
Christ has revealed these things to you.
Oh, good lord, what glory and grace will be yours!"
15   Anno took it very much to heart
that he had to return to earth.
If things had been different just then
he would not have left the kingdom of paradise for all the world,
so great is the joy of heaven.
20   Young and old, we should all turn our thoughts in that direction.
The prince woke up from his sleep.
He knew very clearly what he had to do.
He granted the people of Cologne his favor.
It was their fault entirely that he had been hostile to them.

44   When the time drew near
when God intended to reward him,
he was tormented
just like blessed Job, long ago.
5   He was completely paralyzed
from head to foot.
Then his precious soul departed
from human misery,
from this sick body,
10   and entered eternal paradise.
Earth received the body.
The spirit rose upwards.
We should follow him with our thoughts
to where we will end up at last.

45   Alser dů ci godis antwurte quam,
    cin êwigin ginâdin,
    dů dedde dir heirro edile gemût,
    alsô dir ari sînin iungin důt,
5   sôr si spanin willit ûz vliegin:
    her suêmit ob in ce cierin,
    her wintit sich ûf ci berge,
    daz sint dûnt die iungin gerne.
    alsô woldir uns gespanin,
10   wari wir nâ imi soldin varin.
    her zoigit uns hînidine,
    wilich lebin sî in himile.
    ci demi gravi, dâ sini woltin dôt havin,
    dâ worhtir scône ceichin:
15   die sîchin unti die crumbe,
    dî wurdin dâ gesunte.

46   Arnolt hiez ein vollin gût kneht;
    der havit einin vogitman, hiez Volpreht,
    der durch werltlîche sculde
    virlôs sînis heirrin hulte.
5   dů bigonder godi missitrûwin,
    helphe sůhter an din tiuvil:
    her kós vn imi ci vogite
    wider Arnolde.
    einis âbindis gînc her einin ganc
10   nâ sînimo rosse, einis veldis lanc.
    dâ irschein imi der tiuvil offene.
    her virbôt imi alle Cristis é,
    vnt her nîmanni daz ni sagite,
    wî her un gesîn havite.
15   her quad, giwûge hers eincheinim manne,
    her cibrêchin ci stukkelîni allin;
    wolter avir imi volgin,
    sô hetter imi gewissin holtin.
    mit drón unti mit geheizan
20   virleitter dů den tumbin man,
    daz her gelîz sich cis vîantis trûwin.
    daz ward imi sint ci rûwin.

45   When he came into the presence
      of the everlasting mercy of God,
      the nobly minded lord behaved
      like the eagle when it wants to tempt its young
5   to fly off on their own.
      It soars gloriously over them.
      It circles higher and higher
      so that, later, the young are eager to do the same.
      Thus he wanted to lure us
10   to the place where we should follow after him.
      He showed us down below
      what sort of life there would be in heaven.
      At the grave where they believed him dead
      he performed great miracles.
15   The sick and the lame
      were cured there.

46   There was a most excellent knight named Arnold.
      He had a dependent by the name of Volprecht,
      who had lost the favor of his lord
      on account of secular transgressions.
5   Then he began to lose faith in God.
      He sought help from the Devil.
      He chose him as his protector
      against Arnold.
      One evening he was walking
10   across a field to his horse.
      There the Devil appeared to him openly.
      He forbade him absolutely to follow the gospel of Christ
      and ordered him not to tell anyone
      that he had seen him.
15   He said that if he told anyone at all
      he would tear him up into tiny pieces.
      However, if he obeyed him
      he would have a reliable friend in him.
      With threats and with promises
20   the Devil led the foolish man astray
      so that he gave in to his promises.
      Later he regretted having done so.

47   Des andren tagis her mit Arnolde reit.
       dis tiuvilis geheizi was her vili gemeit.
       mit misselîchin redin her dar zû quam,
       daz her godis bigonde virlouchinan.
5   godis heiligin bigonder lasterin —
       daz nîman nisolti gebaldin — ,
       vnzi dů der vili tumbe man
       bigondi lasterin seint Annin.
       her quad, dad her iz al wol irkante,
10   iz wêr al triugeheit unti scante;
       Anno lebit ié mit suntin.
       wad ceichine her getuon solte?
       dere vrebelîchin schelti
       můster sân intgeltin:
15   dâ cistede sîn ouge winister
       vůr imi ûz als ein wazzer.
       dů der ungeloubige man
       ni wolti sich irkeinnin,
       her niwolti seint Annin sceltin,
20   dů mů̊ste hers mêr intgeltin.
       durch sîn hoibit quam ein slag,
       daz her dir nidiri gelach.
       als ein gescôz daz ouge ceswe
       spreiz ûz imi verre.
25   dů vîl her nidir an did gras,
       her schrei, als imi was.
       harti irquâmin si sich des ubiral,
       si bedditin ci gote in crûcestal.

48   Arnolt hîs drâdi rennin,
       paffen imi dari gewinnin.
       sô vůrtin si in ceinir kirichin.
       si lêrtin un sîni pigihti tûn,
5   vnzi dů der sêregi man
       sent Annin anedingin bigan.
       her bat sînir genâdin,
       daz her den gesunt imi virgâbi.
       michil wunter sâgin
10   alli, dî dů dâ wârin:

47   The next day he was out riding with Arnold.
        He was delighted by the Devil's promise.
        While talking about various things,
        Volprecht went so far as to deny God.
5   He began to revile God's saints,
        which no one should be so bold as to do,
        until this very foolish man
        began to revile St. Anno.
        He said that he knew very well
10   that it was all a shameful deception.
        Anno had always lived in sin.
        What sort of miracles would he be able to perform?
        Volprecht had to pay at once
        for this brazen abuse.
15   Then and there his left eye
        ran out of his face like water.
        When the faithless man
        refused to come to his senses
        and continued to abuse St. Anno
20   he had to pay an even higher price.
        A stroke went through his head
        so that he fell down onto the ground.
        His right eye squirted out of him
        far away like a shot.
25   Then he fell down onto the grass.
        He cried out on account of his condition.
        This terrified people all around.
        They prayed to God with their arms stretched out like crosses.

48   Arnold ordered them all to run quickly
        to fetch priests for him.
        They brought him to a church.
        They urged him to confess his sins
5   until the injured man
        began to place his hope in St. Anno.
        He prayed that Anno might show mercy
        and restore his health to him.
        All those who were there
10   saw a great miracle.

in den îtilin ougistirnin
wûhsin niuwe ougin widere,
daz her sân ci stundin woli gesach.
sô scône ist diu godis craft.

49   Von altin êwin ist daz kunt,
wî sich wîlin ûf tedde der merigrunt,
dů Moyses das liut Israêl
mit trukkenim wegge leite ubir sê
5 ci demi allir bezzistin lante
(des die gůtin ouch sulin waltin):
dâ die becche miliche vluzzin,
diz sůze honig dar inzuschin;
diz olei ûz eime steine sprunge,
10 sân dir bî der sůze brunne;
diz brôt vane himele reginete,
allis gûdis si seide habiten.
mit wuntirlîchin ceichinin
êrete got Moysen, den heiligin,
15 vnz ein sîn selbis suster
bigondimi sprecchin laster.
ô wî starche si dî misilsuht bistûnt,
vnz iri gewegete der brůder gût!
alsô gewegete seint Anno disim man,
20 daz her sîni gesunt gewan,
ci diu daz wir virstûntin
des rîchin godis gůte,
wî her sô lônit unti ricchit,
suaz man sînin holtin spricchit,
25 der sô sůze leidit albihanten
ci demi scônin paradysi lante.

New eyes grew back
in the empty eye sockets
so that he could see perfectly at once.
So magnificent is the power of God.

49   We know from the Old Testament
how the seabed was revealed long ago
when Moses led the people of Israel
on a dry path through the sea
5   into the best of all lands,
which the blessed will also have as theirs,
where the streams flowed with milk,
sweet honey mixed in.
Oil burst forth from a rock,
10   alongside it a spring with fresh water.
Bread rained down from the sky.
They had a sufficiency of all good things.
God honored Moses, the saint,
with marvelous signs
15   until one of his own sisters
started to slander him.
Oh, how painfully she was stricken with leprosy,
until her good brother helped her!
In just that way St. Anno helped this man
20   to regain his health
so that we might understand
the power and goodness of God,
the way he rewards and punishes
whatever anyone says about his servants,
25   those whom he leads so gently and swiftly
into the blessed land of paradise.

DIE KAISERCHRONIK

vv. 247–667

   Die chuonen Rômære
rewelten ainen hêrren,
ain vermezzen helt,

250   von dem daz buoch michil tugent zelt.
vil grôz lop si im sungen;
si santen den helt jungen
ze Dûtiscen landen.
vil wol si inen erchanden:

255   er hêt ain stætigen muot,
en allen wîs was er ein helt guot.
   Do enpfulhen Rômâre
Jûlîô dem hêrren
drîzech tûsint helede

260   mit guotem geserewe.
Jûlîus der hêrre
drîzec tûsent nam er selbe mêre,
want er dâ vor was in Dûtiscen landen
und er ir ellen wol rekande,

265   want er in ir haimilîche was.
dô wesser wol, daz iz nehain frum was.
   Juljus was ain guot kneht:
vil sciere was er gereht,
und ander sîne holden

270   die mit im varen solden.
er kêrte engegen Swâben;
den tet er michel ungenâde.
ze Swâben was dô gesezzen
ain helt vil vermezzen,

275   genant was er Prenne:
er rait im mit her engegene.
   Daz buoch tuot uns kunt:
er vaht mit im drîe stunt
mit offenem strîte.

CHRONICLE OF THE EMPERORS

section that includes passages from the *Annolied*

The brave Romans
chose a general,
a bold warrior, of whom the book
250 on which we have relied relates many accomplishments.
They sang his praises to the sky.
They sent the young hero
to German lands.
They knew him very well.
255 He never wavered in his intentions.
He was an excellent warrior in every regard.
   The Romans entrusted
Julius, the general,
with thirty thousand
260 well-armed warriors.
The general, Julius,
took thirty thousand more on his own
since he had been in German lands previously
and was well acquainted with their valor,
265 since he had been in their confidence.
But he realized that this would not bring him any advantage.
   Julius was an excellent fighter.
He was ready at once,
as were those of his followers
270 who were to accompany him.
He turned towards Swabia.
He treated them very harshly.
At that time a fearless hero
called Prenne
275 held sway in Swabia.
He led an army on horseback against him.
   The book tells us
that he fought with him three times
on the battlefield.

280 si sluogen wunden wîte,
     si frumten manigen bluotigen rant.
     die Swâbe werten wol ir lant,
     unz si Juljus mit minnen
     rebat ze aim teidinge.
285 ir lant si dâ gâben
     in sîne genâde.
     sîn gezelt hiez er slahen dô
     ûf ain berch der heizet Swêrô:
     von dem berge Swêrô
290 sint si alle gehaizen Swâbe,
     ain liut ze râte vollen guot,
     — si sint ouh redespæhe genuoc — ,
     di sih diche des fur nâmen,
     daz si guote reken wæren,
295 wol vertic unt wol wîchaft.
     iedoh betwanc Juljus Cêsar alle ir chraft.
       Die Swâbe rieten Jûlîô,
     er kêrte ûf die Baire,
     dâ vil manich tegen inne saz.
300 Boimunt ir herzoge was,
     sîn pruoder hiez Ingram.
     vil sciere besanten si ir man,
     in kom an der stunt
     vil manic helt junc
305 mit halsperge unt mit prunne.
     si werten sih mit grimme,
     si vâhten mit im ain volcwîc:
     neweder ê noh sît
     gelac nie sô manic helt guot,
310 oder uns liegent diu haideniskon buoch.
     owî wie guote cnehte Baier wâren,
     daz ist in den haidenisken buochen mære.
     dâ liset man inne 'Noricus ensis',
     daz kît ain swert Baierisc.
315 diu swert man dike durch den helm sluoc,
     dem liute was sîn ellen vil guot.
       Diu geslähte der Baiere
     her kômen von Armenje,

280　They slashed open large wounds.
　　　They bloodied many shields.
　　　The Swabians fought valiantly in defense of their land
　　　until Julius, acting as a friend,
　　　invited them to a meeting.
285　At this meeting they entrusted their country
　　　to his mercy.
　　　Afterwards he ordered his tents to be raised
　　　on a mountain called Swero.
　　　They are all called Swabians,
290　from Mt. Swero.
　　　They are a people very good at counsel —
　　　they are also quite eloquent —
　　　who frequently distinguished themselves
　　　as excellent fighters,
295　always ready and warlike.
　　　Nevertheless, Julius Caesar overcame their entire fighting strength.
　　　　The Swabians advised Julius
　　　to turn against Bavaria,
　　　where a great many warriors lived.
300　Their duke was Boimunt.
　　　His brother was called Ingram.
　　　They sent at once for their vassals.
　　　Without delay a large number
　　　of young warriors came to them,
305　bringing hauberks and shirts of mail.
　　　They defended themselves fiercely.
　　　They fought a massed battle with him.
　　　Neither before nor since
　　　have so many fine warriors been slain —
310　or else the books of the heathen are lying to us.
　　　Indeed, there are accounts in the books of the heathen
　　　telling what excellent fighters the Bavarians were.
　　　There you can read about "Noricus ensis."
　　　That means a Bavarian sword.
315　Over and over their swords slashed through each other's helmets.
　　　This people had profited greatly from its bravery.
　　　　The Bavarian tribe
　　　had come from Armenia,

dâ Nôê ûz der arke gie
320 unt daz olzwî von der tûben enphie.
ir zaichen noch diu arka hât
ûf den bergen di dâ haizent Ararât.
den sig den Juljus an den Bairen gewan
den muoser mit pluote sêre geltan.
325 Der Sahsen grimmigez muot
tet im dô laides genuoc.
die liset man daz si wâran
des wunderlîchen Alexanders man,
der ze Babilonje sîn ende genam.
330 dô teilten sîn scaz vier sîne man,
die wolten wesen kunige.
die andern fuoren wîten irre after lante,
unz ir ain teil mit scefmenige
kômen ûf bî der Elbe,
335 dâ duo der site was
daz man diu micheln mezzer hiez sahs,
der di rechen manegez truogen,
dâ mit si di Duringe sluogen.
mit untriwe kômen si in aine sprâche:
340 die Sahsen den fride brâchen.
von den mezzern wassen
sint si noch gehaizen Sahsen.
Cêsar begunde dô nâhen
zu sînen alten mâgen,
345 ze Franken den vil edelen.
ir biderben vorderen
kômen von Trôje der alten
di di Chrîchen zervalten.
Ob ir iz gelouben wellent,
350 daz ih iu wil rehte zellen,
wi des herzogen Ulixes gesinde
ain cyclops vraz in Sicilje,
daz Ulixes mit spiezen wol rach,
do er slâfende im sîn ouge ûz stach.
355 sîn gesclähte dannoh
was in dem walde alsô hôh
sam die tanpoume.

where Noah went forth from the ark
320   and received the olive branch from the dove.
There are still signs of the ark
on the mountains there, which are called Ararat.
Julius had to pay a high price in blood
for his victory over the Bavarians.
325   Next the fury of the Saxons
caused him plenty of trouble.
You can read that they were
followers of the amazing Alexander,
who met his end in Babylon.
330   Subsequently his treasure was divided up
by four of his men who wanted to be king.
The others strayed far and wide, through many lands,
until one group
sailed up the Elbe in a fleet of ships.
335   At that time it was the custom there
to call long knives *sahs*.
The fugitive warriors carried many of these knives,
with which they killed the Thuringians.
They came to a meeting in bad faith.
340   The Saxons broke the truce.
They are still called Saxons
on account of their sharp knives.
    Caesar then approached
the most noble Franks,
345   who were his relatives from long ago.
Their valiant forebears
had left the ancient city of Troy,
which was leveled by the Greeks.
    I hope you will believe me
350   when I tell you the truth concerning
the troops led by Ulysses.
They were eaten by a cyclops in Sicily,
which Ulysses avenged by poking the cyclops's eye out
with a spear while he was sleeping.
355   At that time the race of the cyclops
was as tall as the fir trees
in the forest.

an der stirne habeten si vorne ain ouge.
nû hât si got von uns vertriben hinnen
360   in daz gewälde enehalb Indîe.
    Trôjâni vuoren in dirre werlte
vil wîten irre after lande,
unz Elenus ain verherter man
des kuonen Hectoris witewen genam,
365   mit der er ze Crîchen
besaz sîner vîande rîche.
Anthênor vuor dannen,
duo Trôja was zergangen,
er stiphte Mantowe
370   und ain ander haizet Padowe.
Enêas ervaht Rômiskiu lant,
da er ain sû mit drîzec wîzen jungen vant.
Franko gesaz mit den sînen
niden bî dem Rîne:
375   den Rîn hêt er vur daz mer.
dâ wuohsen elliu Frenkisken her.
diu wurden Cêsari undertân,
iedoh was iz im harte sorcsam.
    Juljus worhte dô bî Rîne
380   die sedelhove sîne:
Diuze ain stat guote,
Bocbarte der ze huote;
Andernâche ain state guote,
Ingelnhaim der zu huote;
385   Magenze ain stat guote,
Oppenhaim ir ze huote.
duo worhte der helt snel
ingegen Magenze ain castel.
ain bruke worht er dâ uber Rîn:
390   wi maht diu burch baz gezieret sîn?
diu versanc sît in des Rînes grunde.
daz chom von den sunden,
daz Magenzâre nie nehaim ir hêrren
mit triwen mite wâren.
395   Dannoh stuont Triere
mit michelen êren.

They had one eye in front on their forehead.
Now God has driven them far away from us
360   into the forests on the other side of India.
　　The Trojans wandered about the earth,
straying far and wide through many lands,
until Helenus, who had been defeated,
married the widow of brave Hector,
365   with whom he took possession
of his enemies' kingdom in Greece.
Antenor had left Troy
when it was destroyed.
He founded Mantua
370   and another city called Padua.
Aeneas won by force the lands of Rome,
where he found a sow with thirty white piglets.
Franko settled down with his followers
along the Rhine.
375   He took the Rhine in place of the sea.
That is where the Franks increased in number.
They became subject to Caesar,
although it cost him much trouble.
　　That was when Julius built
380   his residences along the Rhine:
Deutz, an excellent place,
with Boppard to guard it;
Andernach, an excellent place,
with Ingelheim to guard it;
385   Mainz, an excellent place,
with Oppenheim to guard it.
Then the valiant warrior built
a castle near Mainz.
He built a bridge across the Rhine there.
390   What better ornament for a city could there be?
Later it sank to the bottom of the Rhine.
That was caused by the sinfulness
of the people of Mainz, who never
remained true to any of their lords.
395   　Trier, on the other hand,
enjoyed great power.

si stuont an einem ende
in Franken lande,
in Bellicâ Gallîâ.
400 vil kuone wâren si dâ,
si werten wol ir lant,
unz Jûlîus der wîgant
mit listen in die burch an gewan:
daz machet der vurste Lâbîân.
405   Nû wil ih iu sagen wie ez kom,
daz Juljus Triere gewan.
si werten sih dâ vor, daz ist wâr,
mêr denne vier jâr.
in der burc wâren dô zwêne
410 gewaltige hêrren,
der eine hiez Dulzmâr,
der ander Signâtôr.
di begunden sih zwaien,
under in ze strîten
415 umbe di grôzen hêrscaft
diu ze Triere was in der stat.
Signâtor wart Cêsaris man
unt sîn bruoder Lâbîân.
von ir ræten iz bechom
420 daz Dulzmâr wart erslagen
und daz Juljus Triere uberwant.
er vant dar inne manigen tûrlîchen wîgant.
   Die wîle di hêrren
mit triwen samt wâren,
425 wie dike si rieten
daz si wider den chaiser tæten
mit grimmem volcwîge!
do bestuont si der zwîvel:
vil michil volc ze scanden gât
430 dâ si der zwîvel bestât,
di dâ wol sint ainmuote
die werdent dike stâte.
durch zwîvel der hêrren
sô nam in Juljus alle ir êre.
435   Alse Juljus in Triere chom,

It was situated in the outer reaches
of the land of the Franks,
in Belgian Germany.
400 Those who lived there were very brave.
They defended their land valiantly
until the hero, Julius,
won the city from them by a stratagem.
This was the work of prince Labian.
405   Now I will tell you how it came to pass
that Julius won Trier.
It is true that they had defended themselves
against him for more than four years.
At that time there were two
410 powerful lords in the city.
One was called Dulzmar,
the other Signator.
They fell out
and began to fight each other
415 for the great power there was
in ruling the city of Trier.
Signator became Caesar's man
along with his brother Labian.
As they advised,
420 Dulzmar was killed
and Julius overcame Trier.
Within the city he found many excellent fighters.
   As long as the lords
remained united in good faith,
425 they kept planning
to attack the emperor
with a furious massed battle.
But then they were beset by distrust.
Many a people suffers disgrace
430 where it is beset by distrust,
while those who are truly of one mind
are likely to endure.
The distrust of the lords enabled Julius
to deprive them of all their power.
435   When Julius entered Trier

si wânten, si hêten alle den ir lîp verlorn.
Cêsar was edele unt kuone,
diu burch dûht in veste unt scône;
von diu liez er die hêrren
440 in den selben êren
dâ er si vor inne vant.
die burc bevalh er in ir aller gewalt,
den oberisten hêrren
den lêh er guotiu lêhen,
445 den kuonisten gab er daz golt;
die wâren im alle willich unt holt.
die aller ermisten diet
die liez er âne gebe niet.
daz lêrt in sîn diemuot.
450 Cêsar was milt unde guot,
vil michel was sîn sin.
alse lange wonete er under in
unz im alle Dûtiske hêrren
willic wâren ze sînen êren.
455 Duo Juljus wider ze Rôme san,
si newolten sîn niht enphâhen,
si sprâchen, daz er durch sîn gail
ir heres hête verlorn ain michel tail,
unt daz er ze Dûtisken landen
460 ân ir urloup ze lange wære bestanden.
mit zorne er wider wante
ze Dûtiscem lante.
er sante nâh allen den hêrren
di in Dûtiscem rîche wâren,
465 er chlagete in allen sîne nôt,
er bôt in sîn golt rôt,
er sprach, swaz er in ze laide hête getân,
er wolte sis wol ergezzan.
Do si vernâmen sînen willen,
470 duo samenten sih die snellen.
ûzer Gallîa unt ûzer Germanje
kômen scar manige
mit scînenden helmen,
mit vesten halspergen.

they all supposed they would lose their lives.
Caesar was noble and brave.
The citadel seemed strong and well-built to him.
For this reason he let the lords retain
440 the same dignity
that they had enjoyed before.
He placed the city under their jurisdiction.
He bestowed desirable fiefs
on the greatest lords.
445 He gave gold to the bravest.
They were all devoted to him and ready to do his bidding.
Nor did he leave the poorest people
without gifts.
His humility taught him this.
450 Caesar was generous and noble.
His intelligence was great.
He remained among them
until all the German lords
were ready to serve his glory.
455   When Julius headed back to Rome
the Romans did not want to receive him.
They said that he had lost a large part
of their army through his own arrogance
and that he had remained too long
460 in German lands without their permission.
In anger he returned
to German lands
and summoned all the lords
who were in the German province.
465 He lamented his trouble to them all.
He offered them his red gold.
He said he wanted to compensate them
for any harm he had done them.
   When they heard what he had in mind
470 the eager warriors gathered together.
Many troops came
from Gaul and Germania,
bringing shining helmets
and strong coats of mail.

475 si laiten manigen scônen sciltes rant:
als ain fluot vuoren si ze Rôme in daz lant.
do iz Rômære gesâhen,
wie harte si erchômen!
do ervorht im vil manic man,

480 duo Juljus mit Tûtiscer rîterscephte sô hêrlîchen chom
unt si sâhen scînen
die braiten scar sîne,
fan unte borten;
ir lîbes si harte vorhten.

485 Rigidus Câto und Pompêjus
die rûmten alle Rômisken hûs,
unt aller senâtus:
mit sorgen fluhen si dar ûz.
er vuor in nâch jagende,

490 vil wîten slahende.
Pompêjus flôh an daz mer,
er gewan daz aller chreftigest her
daz in der werlte ie dehain man
zu sîner helfe gewan.

495   Juljus strebet in engegene,
iedoh mit minre menige.
durh der Dûtiscen trôst
wie vast er in nâh zôh!
dâ wart daz hertiste volcwîc,

500 als daz buoch vor chît,
daz in disem mergarten
ie gefrumt mahte werden.
owî wi di sarringe chlungen,
dâ diu march zesamene sprungen!

505 herhorn duzzen,
peche pluotes fluzzen.
da belach manich braitiu scar
mit bluote berunnen alsô gar.
Jûlîus den sig nam,

510 Pompêjus chûme intran;
er flôh in Egipten lant:
dannen tet er niemer mêr widerwant.
Pompêjus reslagen lac,

475 They brought many excellent shields.
They streamed into the land of Rome like a flood.
How the Romans were terrified
when they saw what was happening!
Many men were afraid
480 when Julius arrived in splendor with the German knights
and they saw such a vast host
shining in the sun,
with their standards and their shield straps.
They were very afraid they would lose their lives.
485 Rigidus Cato and Pompey
and the entire Senate
all abandoned their Roman home.
They fled the city in fear.
Julius pursued them,
490 striking them down everywhere.
Pompey fled to the sea.
He gathered the mightiest army
that anyone in the world ever assembled
in his own cause.
495   Julius pushed towards them,
but with a smaller force.
With the help of the Germans
he pursued them very closely.
According to the book
500 it was the most brutal massed battle
that two armies would ever fight
against each other in this world.
Alas, how the armor resounded
whenever the war horses charged together!
505 Battle trumpets filled the air.
Blood flowed in streams.
A vast expanse of troops lay there
completely covered with blood.
Julius won the victory.
510 Pompey barely escaped.
He fled into the land of Egypt
and never returned again.
Pompey was beaten.

Juljus Cêsar in sît rach.

515   Duo frouwete sih der junge man,
daz er diu rîche elliu under sih gewan.
er fuor dô mit michelem gewalte
wider ze Rôme swie er wolte.
Rômâre in dô wol enphiengen —
520 si begunden irrizen den hêrren.
daz vunden si im aller êrist ze êren,
want er aine habete den gewalt
der ê was getailet sô manicvalt.
den site hiez er ze êren
525 alle Dûtisce man lêren.

  In den zîten iz gescach
dannen der wîssage Dânîêl dâ vor sprach,
daz der chunic Nabuchodonosor sîne troume sagete
die er gesehen habete:
530 wie vier winde
in dem mere vuoren vehtende
unt ûz dem mer giengen
vier tier wilde.
diu bezaichent vier chunige rîche,
535 die alle dise werlt solten begrîfen.

  Daz êrste tier was ain liebarte;
der vier arenvetech habete,
der bezaichinet den Chrîchisken Alexandrum,
der mit vier hern vuor after lande,
540 unz er der werlt ende rechande.
mit zwain grîfen
vuorter sich selben zuo den luften,
in einem glasevazze
liez er sich in daz mer fram.
545 nâch im wurfen sîn ungetrûwe man
die keten alsô fraissam.
si sprâchen: 'nû dû gerne sihest wunder,
nû sizzi iemer an des meres grunde.'
  Duo sah der wunderlîche man
550 ain tier vur sich gân
aines tages ze prîme
unz an den dritten tach ze nône,

Julius Caesar obtained satisfaction for him later.
515   The young man rejoiced then
since he had brought every kingdom under his control.
Next he turned back towards Rome
with a mighty force, just as he wished.
This time the Romans received him well.
520   They began to address their ruler with *ihr*.
They thought this up to honor him, first of all,
since he alone held the power
that previously had been distributed among so many.
He had this custom taught
525   to all the German men as an honor.
      At that time those things came to pass
that the prophet Daniel had foretold of old,
which King Nebuchadnezzar said
he had seen in his dream:
530   that four winds
moved clashing through the sea
and four wild beasts
went forth from the sea.
They signify four mighty kings
535   who were to possess the entire world.
      The first animal was a leopard
that had four eagle wings.
It signifies Alexander of Greece
who, with four armies, marched through many lands
540   until he saw the end of the world.
He transported himself into the air
with two griffins.
He had himself lowered down into the sea
in a glass container.
545   His faithless men cast
the fearsome chains after him.
They said: "Since you like to see marvelous things,
you can sit on the ocean floor forever."
      One day this amazing man
550   saw a creature pass before him
from prime until the ninth hour
of the third day.

daz was ein grôz wunder;
vil dike walzit iz umbe.
555 duo gedâhte der listege man,
ob er ze dem lîbe trôst solte hân.
mit sîn selbes pluote
daz scarfe mer er gruozte.
als diu fluot des pluotes enphant,
560 si warf in wider ûz an daz lant.
er kom wider in sîn rîche;
vil wol enphiengen in die Chrîchen.
vil manic wunder relait der selbe man,
ain dritteil er der werlte under sih gewan.

565 Daz ander tier was ain pere wilde,
der habete drîvalde zende.
der bezaichenet driu kunincrîche,
diu wider aim solten grîfen.
der pere was alsô fraissam:
570 von mensken sinne nemaht er niemer werden zam.
Daz dritte ain fraislich eber was,
den tiurlîchen Juljum bezaichenet daz.
der selbe eber zehen horn truoc,
dâ mit er sîne vîande alle nider sluoc.

575 Juljus bedwanch elliu lant,
si dienten elliu sîner hant.
wol bezeichenet uns daz wilde swîn
daz daz rîche ze Rôme sol iemer frî sîn.
Daz vierde tier was ain lewin,
580 iz hête mennisclîchen sin,
iz hête mennisken ougen unt munt:
sulhes tieres newart uns ê niht kunt.
im wuohs ain horn gegen dem himele,
die sternen vâhten im ingegene.

585 daz bezeichinet aver den Antichrist,
der noh in die werlt kunftich ist,
den got mit sîner gewelte
hin ze der helle sol senden.
der troum alsô regienc
590 als in der wîssage Dânîêl besciet.
Juljus di triskamere ûf prach,

That was a great marvel.
It kept rolling around him in circles.
555   Then the clever man began to think about
how he could come away with his life.
With his own blood
he irritated the rough sea.
When the water sensed the blood
560   it cast him back out onto land.
He returned to his kingdom.
The Greeks gave him a very warm welcome.
This man experienced a great many amazing things.
He gained control of a third of the world.
565   The second animal was a wild bear
which had three rows of teeth.
It signifies three kingdoms
which were to attack another kingdom.
The bear was very dangerous.
570   Human intelligence could never tame it.
      The third was a fearsome boar.
It stands for the extraordinary Julius.
This boar had ten horns,
with which it cast down all its enemies.
575   Julius conquered every country.
They all rendered service to his power.
The wild boar signifies to us clearly
that the Roman Empire will always remain free.
      The fourth animal was a lioness.
580   It had human intelligence.
It had human eyes and a mouth.
We had never heard of such an animal before.
One of its horns grew towards heaven.
The stars fought against it.
585   It signifies the Antichrist,
who is still to come into this world,
whom almighty God
will send down to hell.
The dream came to pass
590   as the prophet Daniel had interpreted it.
      Julius broke open the treasury

er vant dar inne michelen scaz.
er gebete Dûtisken holden
mit silber unt mit golde.
595   von diu wâren Dûtiske man
ze Rôme ie liep unt lobesam.
diu rîche er mit michelem gewalte habete
die wîle daz er lebete,
daz buoch saget uns vur wâr:
600   niewan fiunf jâr.
Rômâre in ungetrûwelîche sluogen,
sîn gebaine si ûf ain irmensûl begruoben.
   Alse Juljus wart erslagen,
Augustus daz rîche nâh im gewan,
605   von sîner swester was er geborn.
duo er ze rihter wart erkorn,
swie er got niene vorhte,
iedoh er fride worhte
in allen sînen rîchen
610   gewunnen si nie nehainen sämilîchen.
an den stunden,
swelhe in dem rîche wâren gevangen ode gebunden
ode in karkære gestôzen,
die hiez der kunic ûz lâzen.
615   der kuninc vil hêre
er gebôt dannoh mêre:
er hiez scrîben allen disen umberinc,
baidiu muoter unde chint,
baidiu wîp unde man,
620   iegilîchez muose varn
swannen ez geborn was.
daz liet kundet uns daz:
alle die ir hêrren wâren entrunnen
den newolt er des rîches niht gunnen.
625   aines tages hiez er der fremeden slahen,
sô wir daz buoch hôren sagen,
mêr denne drîzec tûsent lîbe,
manne unde wîbe.
   Cêsar Augustus,
630   duo gewarf er alsus:

and found a huge treasure inside.
He bestowed silver and gold
on the devoted Germans.
595   For this reason German men
were always welcome and much praised in Rome.
He ruled the empire with great might
for as long as he lived.
The book tells us truly
600   that that was only five years.
The Romans murdered him treacherously
and buried his remains on top of a high column.
   When Julius had been killed
Augustus took possession of the empire after him.
605   He was the child of Caesar's sister.
Even though he did not fear God in the least,
after he had been chosen to be ruler
he established peace
throughout all his realms
610   such as they achieved at no other time.
At that time the king decreed
that anyone who had been captured or bound
or thrown into prison
anywhere in the empire be freed.
615   That most exalted king
ordered something else as well.
He decreed that all the earth should be recorded,
whether mother or child,
whether man or woman.
620   Each person had to travel
to the place where he or she was born.
The song tells us that he did not want to
allow in the empire any of those
who had run away from their lords.
625   One day, so the book tells us,
he ordered more than 30,000
foreigners, men and women,
to be slain.
   Then Caesar Augustus
630   did the following:

er hiez im wurken aver sâ
ain wâge diu hiez didragmâ,
er gebôt in bî dem halse,
si gêbin si ze cinse
635 — arm unde rîche
di dâ wâren in sînem rîche —,
diu fier phenninge wac.
der cins stuont unz an den tac
daz der wâre hailant
640 von himele wart gesant
uns allen ze trôste,
der uns von dem cinse relôste.
  Agrippâ wart duo gesant,
daz er ze Rîne berihte daz lant.
645 aine burch worhte dô der hêrre
Rômæren ze êren.
den namen gab er ir sâ:
er hiez si Agrippînâ,
Colonjâ ist si nû genant,
650 si zieret elliu Frenkiskiu lant.
Mezze stiphte ain sîn man
Mêtîus geheizan.
Triere was ain burch alt,
die zierte Rômære gewalt,
655 dannen si den wîn verre
santen under der erde
in stainen rinnen,
den hêrren al ze minnen
di ze Cholne wâren sedelhaft.
660 michel was der Rômære chraft.
  Augustus der vil mære man —
Augustâ hât noh von im namen —
vil gewalteclîche beriht er Rôme.
jâ truoc er die corône,
665 daz saget daz buoch vur wâr,
sehs unde fiunfzic jâr,
drî mânode dar ubere.

he had a scale made for himself
that was called "double drachma."
He ordered on pain of death
that both the rich and the poor
635 who were in his empire
pay tribute
that weighed four pennies.
The tribute remained in effect until the day
when the true savior
640 was sent from heaven
to comfort us all,
who freed us from the tribute.
   Then Agrippa was dispatched
to bring order to the province along the Rhine.
645 Once there this general constructed a city
to the glory of the Romans.
He named it at once.
He called it Agrippina.
Now it is called Cologne.
650 It brings glory to all the lands of the Franks.
Metz was founded by one of his followers
called Metius.
Trier was an old city,
embellished by the power of the Romans,
655 from which they sent wine
in stone conduits
a long way underground
out of devotion to the lords
who resided in Cologne.
660 The power of the Romans was great.
   Augustus, the celebrated man —
Augsburg still preserves his name —
ruled Rome with great might.
Indeed, he wore the crown,
665 as the book tells us truly,
three months more
than fifty-six years.

DAS LOB SALOMONS

1   Inclita lux mundi,
        du dir habis in dinir kundi
        erdin undi lufti
        unde alli himilcrefti,
5   du sendi mir zi mundi,
        daz ich eddilichin deil muzzi kundin
        di gebi vili sconi,
        di du deti Salomoni,
        di manicfaltin wisheit:
10   ubir dich mendit du cristinheit.

2   Salomon Davidis sun was,
        du richi er sit nach imo bisaz.
        durh sinis vatir sculdi
        gond imo got sinir huldi.
5   er sprach, daz er gebiti,
        swedir so er wolti,
        richtum odir wisheit.
        durch di sini vrumicheit
        er gihohit in so werdi
10   ubir alli, di dir warin an dir erdi.

3   Der herro sich bidachti,
        zi goti er keriti:
        'herro, du weist vil woli,
        al wi michil lut ich biwarin sol.
5   du machi mich so wisi,
        daz ich richti so dir gilichi.
        wil du mir den wistum gebin,
        so mag ich immir erhafti lebin.
        daz ist dir allir meisti list,
10   so giwin ich swaz mir lib ist.'

4   Du stimmi sprach dannin
        zi demo kuninclichen manni:

In Praise of Solomon

1 *Inclita lux mundi*,
 you who comprehend
 earth and air
 and all the powers of heaven,
5 grant that my mouth might
 proclaim at least in some measure
 that most splendid gift,
 the great wisdom,
 that you bestowed on Solomon.
10 Christendom rejoices in you.

2 Solomon was the son of David.
 He ruled his kingdoms after him.
 God granted him his favor
 on his father's account.
5 He said he would give him
 whichever he desired,
 wealth or wisdom.
 On account of his worthiness
 he exalted him magnificently
10 above all who walked the earth.

3 The king considered what to do.
 He turned to God.
 "Lord, you know very well
 what a great multitude of people are in my care.
5 Make me so wise
 that I might rule as you would.
 If you deign to grant me wisdom,
 then I will always be able to live with honor.
 That is the most difficult skill of all.
10 With it I will gain whatever I wish."

4 Then the voice of God spoke
 to the king:

'nu du virkorn hast den richtum
undi griffi an den wistum,
5   nu wil ich dich merin
mid michilin erin.
ich machi dinin giwalt
wit undi manincfalt,
daz man dinin gilichin
10   nimag findin in allin disin richin.'

5   David ein duirir wigant,
der alli sini not ubirwant,
der bigondi also werdi
allir erist her in erdi
5   goti ein hus zimmiron:
des giwanner michilin lon.
daz volworhti sit Salomon,
er zirit iz mit michilin eron,
mit manigir slachti wunnin
10   demo himilischen kunigi zi minnin.

6   Ein herro hiz Heronimus
(sin scripft zelit uns sus),
der heti ein michil wundir
uzzir einim buchi vundin,
5   uzzir Archely
(daz habint noch di Crichi),
wi in Hiersalem giscach
michilis wundiris gimach.
ein wurm wuchs dar inni,
10   der irdranc alli di brunni,
di dir in der burch warin;
die cisternin wurdin leri:
des chomin di luiti
in eini vil starchi noti.

7   Salmon der was richi.
er ded so wislichi,
er hiz daz luit zu gan,
vullin eini cisternam

"Since you have disdained riches
and seized on wisdom
5   I will raise you
to great glory.
I will extend your power
in many ways, far and wide
so that your equal will not be found
10   in all the kingdoms on earth."

5   David, an excellent warrior,
who had overcome every obstacle he faced,
was the first person on earth
to build a house for God
5   in such a splendid fashion.
For this he gained a great reward.
Subsequently Solomon completed it.
He decorated it sumptuously,
with much to delight the eyes,
10   for love of the heavenly king.

6   A highborn man named Jerome,
whose writings tell us this,
discovered a great marvel
in a book,
5   in the *Archaiologia*
(which the Greeks still possess)
how a great marvel
occurred in Jerusalem.
A dragon lived there.
10   He drank up all the springs
in the city.
The cisterns were emptied.
As a result the people
were sorely afflicted.

7   Solomon was mighty.
He acted very wisely.
He had people go
and fill a cistern

5   meddis undi winis,
dis allir bezzistin lidis.
do er iz alliz uz gitranc,
ich weiz er in slaffinti bant.
daz was ein michil gotis craft,
10   daz imo der wurm zu sprach.
der vreissami drachi,
zi Salmoni sprach er:
'herro, nu virla mich,
so biwisin ich dich
15   einir vili michilin erin
zi dinim munsteri:
du wurchist in enim jari,
wil du mirz giloubin,
daz du snidis minu bant,
20   vil manigir claftirin lanc.'

8   Salomon sprach do
vil wislichin dir zu:
'nu sagi mirz vil schiri,
odir ich heizzi dich virlisin.'
5   der wurm sprach imo zu:
'ein dir gat in Libano,
daz heiz du dir giwinnin,
di adirin bringin.
ich sagi dir rechti wi du du:
10   dar uz werchi eini snuir,
du wirt scarf undi was,
du snidit als ein scarsachs
uffi den marmilstein.
vil ebini muzzer inzwei,
15   swi so dir lib ist.'
der kunic vrowit sich des.

9   Salomon was richi,
er det so wislichi:
er hiz imo snidin du bant
undi virbot imo du lant.
5   do vur er zi waldi

5   with mead and wine,
and the very best spiced wine.
I know that when the dragon had drunk it dry
Solomon tied him up while he was sleeping.
It was through the fullness of God's power
10   that the dragon spoke to him.
The fearsome dragon
said to Solomon:
"My lord, if you set me free now
then I will tell you
15   about something quite glorious
for your temple.
If you believe me
and cut my bonds,
you will advance your work in a single year
20   by a great many fathoms."

8   Solomon responded
very wisely:
"Now tell me about this at once,
or I will have you destroyed."
5   The dragon said to him:
"There is an animal that lives in Lebanon.
Have it caught for you.
Have the veins brought.
I will tell you what you should do.
10   Make a cord out of them.
It will be keen and sharp.
It will cut through marble
like a razor.
The stone will be divided very cleanly in two,
15   just as you wish."
The king was glad of that.

9   Solomon was mighty.
He acted very wisely.
He had the dragon's bonds cut
and ordered him out of the country.
5   Then he traveled into the forest

mid allin sinin holdin.
er vant daz dir in Lybano,
zi steti jagit erz do.
do jagit erz alli
10   dri tagi volli.
do er daz dir do giwan,
do was er ein vro man.
er hiz iz imo giwinnin,
di adirin bringin.
15   von du wart daz hus ze Hiersalem
giworcht ani alliz isin.

10   Do was daz hus richi
giworcht mid michilin vlizzi.
di wenti warin marmilstein vil wiz,
daz himiliz undi der estirich.
5   dar inni hangitin sconi
di guldinin cronin.
da was inni lux undi claritas,
suzzi stanc suavitas.
daz was also lussam,
10   so iz demo himilischin kunigi woli gizam.

11   Du lagil undi du hantvaz,
di viole undi du lichtvaz,
du rouchvaz undi du cherzistal,
daz roti golt was iz al.
5   daz bivalch man den ewartin,
di dir got vorchtin,
di dir dagis undi nachtis
phlagin gotis ammichtis.
daz wart also gordinot,
10   als iz der wisi Salomon gibot.

12   Ein kunigin chom sundir
zi Salmoni durch wundir.
du brachti michilin scaz,
thymiama undi opes,
5   des edilin gistenis

with all his retainers.
He found the animal in Lebanon.
At once he set about hunting it.
He hunted it
10   for three whole days.
Once he had captured the animal
he was a happy man.
He had it procured for himself
and had the veins brought.
15   This is how the temple in Jerusalem
was constructed without any iron.

10   That magnificent structure
was constructed with great care.
The walls were whitest marble
as were the ceiling and the floor.
5   Beautiful golden chandeliers
hung within.
Inside were *lux* and *claritas*,
sweet smells, *suavitas*.
It was so pleasing
10   it would be suitable for the heavenly king.

11   The vessels and basins,
the cups and the lamps,
the censers and the candelabra
were all of red gold.
5   These were entrusted to the priests,
who feared God
and celebrated God's office
day and night.
Everything was arranged
10   as wise Solomon had ordained.

12   From the south a queen came to Solomon
on account of the marvels.
She brought a great treasure,
thymiama and *opes*,
5   and precious stones

grozzis undi cleinis.
su was ein vrowi vil rich,
iri gebi was vil kuniclich.

13   Du buoch zelint uns vili giwis,
in sinim hovi worchti man einin disc
mid silbirin stollin.
den disc trugins alli,
5   in allin virin sin uf hubin,
vur den kunic si in trugin;
dar obi goumit er sconi.
daz holz kom von Lybano.
demo der wistum si cleini,
10   der virnemi waz du zali meini.

14   In sinim hovi was vil michil zucht,
da was inni allis guotis ginucht;
sin richtum imo vil woli schein.
sin stul was gut helphinbein,
5   woli gidreit undi irgrabin,
mid dim goldi was er bislagin.
sechs gradi gingin dir zu.
zwelf gummin dinotin imo du.
dru tusint maniger erin,
10   di giwist er alli mid sinir leri.

15   Sin dinist daz was vesti,
so min demo kunigi solti gebin sin ezzin.
di scuzzilin undi di nepphi,
di woli gisteinitin chophi,
5   daz was alliz guldin.
si achden sinen huldin.
nihinis dinistmannis niwart min
. . . .
. . . dinotin gizoginlichi,
10   also gibot Salomon dir richi.

both large and small.
She was a ruler of great power.
Her gifts were appropriate for a king.

13   In books we can read for a certainty
        that a table had been built at his court
        with silver supports.
        They carried this table as a unit.
5   They lifted it up at all four corners.
        They carried it before the king.
        He ate his meals on it in splendor.
        The wood came from Lebanon.
        Those who are deficient in wisdom
10   should hear what this means.

14   There was great refinement at his court.
        There there was a sufficiency of all good things.
        His riches shone upon him brilliantly.
        His throne was of fine ivory,
5   beautifully turned and carved
        and studded with gold.
        Six *gradi* led up to it.
        Twelve men served him then.
        Three thousand of great renown,
10   he instructed all of them with his teaching.

15   The king received exacting service
        when it was time to bring him his meals.
        The bowls and the cups,
        the bejeweled goblets
5   were all golden.
        They strove to gain his favor.
        There was not a single servant
        . . . .
        . . . served properly
10   as the mighty Solomon ordained.

16   Sin dinist daz was vesti:
       so der kunic solti gan zi resti,
       sechzic irwelitir gnechti
       di muosin sin girechti.
  5   der helidi igilich
       druc sin swert umbi sich,
       di dir in soltin biwachtin
       zi iglichin nachtin.
       von similichir ginozschaf
 10   vil michil was sin herschaf.

17   Do chom du gotis stimmi
       zi demo kuniclichin manni;
       der wistum imo zu vloz.
       er niwissi an dir erdi sinin ginoz,
  5   der imo gilich wari
       in sinir vrambairi.
       alliz an imo gizirit was,
       in Hiersalem militaris potestas.

18   Do suz rechti virnam,
       vil harti su sin irchom.
       su sprach 'woli dich, kunic Salomon,
       in dimo hovi ist vil schoni.
  5   vil sælic sint du kint,
       du dir in dinimo dinisti sint.
       dinis wistumis han ich irvundin
       mer danni mir iman mochti irkundin.
       kunic, nu wis gisundi,
 10   ich wil heim zi landi.'

19   Salmon der was heri.
       er hiz vur tragin gebi vil meiri
       des edilin gisteinis,
       grozzis undi cleinis.
  5   mid allin erin hizzer si biwarin,
       er li si vrolichin von imo varin;
       vil minniclichi su von imo irwant,
       er vrumit si ubir daz meri in iri lant.

16   The king received exacting service.
When it was time for him to go to bed
sixty select warriors
were required to attend him.
5   Each of the valiant knights
who were supposed to guard him
every night
carried a sword at his side.
Because he had such companions
10   his dominion was very great.

17   The voice of God
reached the king.
Wisdom poured into him.
He did not know anyone on earth
5   who could equal him
in magnificence.
Everything about him had been made splendid,
in Jerusalem *militaris potestas*.

18   When she understood this fully
she was filled with awe of him.
She said, "Hail, King Solomon,
your court is filled with splendor.
5   Those children are very fortunate
who are in your service.
I have discovered more wisdom in you
than I ever encountered in anyone.
King, stay well.
10   I wish to return home to my country."

19   Solomon was great.
He had very fine gifts brought forth,
gems
large and small.
5   He had every honor bestowed on her.
He let her depart from him with gladness.
She turned from him very lovingly.
He had her brought across the sea to her country.

20   Der kunic bizeichinot den got,
        der disi werilt hat gibilidot,
        in des giwalt alliz daz stat,
        daz daz gistirni umbi gat.
5   imo dinint vil vro
        VIIII chori der eingili:
        di lobint in mid allir macht.
        in simo hovi niwirt nimmir nacht,
        da ist inni daz ewigi licht,
10   des niwirt hini vurdir ziganc nicht.

21   Du kunigin, so ich iz virnemin kan,
        bizeihinot ecclesiam.
        du sol wesin sin brut,
        di minnit er dougin undi ubirlut.
5   ich wæni, simo gimehilot si
        in communionem dei.
        du sol imo gilichin
        in dugintin richlichi,
        du sol giberin du kint,
10   du dir got selbi ginennit sint.

22   Di dinistmin, so ich iz virnemin kan,
        bizeichnont bischoflichi man,
        di dinunt imo in plichti.
        daz lut soltin si birichtin,
5   si soltin lerin di cristinheit
        truwi undi warheit,
        mid werchin irvullin
        daz si demo luti vori zellin.
        si sulin vur den vroni disc
10   goti bringin hostiam laudis.

23   Bi Salmonis zitin
        was sulich vridi undir din lutin,
        swelich enti dir man wolti varin,
        niheinis urlougis wart man giwari.
5   di heriverti warin stilli,
        do dagitin di helidi snelli.

20   The king signifies God,
who formed this world,
who has power over everything
within the compass of the stars.
5   Nine choirs of angels
serve him with great gladness.
They praise him with all their might.
In his court night never falls.
The eternal light shines there,
10   which will never grow dim forevermore.

21   The queen, as I understand it,
signifies *ecclesia*.
She will be his bride.
He loves her secretly and openly.
5   I believe that she is married to him
in communionem dei.
She should resemble him
in fullness of virtue.
She should bear the children
10   who are promised to God.

22   The servants, as I understand it,
signify bishops.
They serve him devotedly.
They should guide people.
5   They should teach Christians
faithfulness and truth
and should realize in their own actions
the instruction they give the people.
They should bring *hostiam laudis*
10   to God at the Lord's table.

23   In the time of Solomon
there was such peace among all peoples
that no matter where one traveled
one never encountered any war.
5   Military campaigns ceased.
Valiant warriors were silent.

niheinis urlougis wart man giphacht,
man nistillit iz alliz mid sinir craft,
als iz got selbi gibot.
10   rex pacificus do richsoti.

24   Salomon der was heri,
sin richtum was vil meri.
der des himilis walti
undi daz luit suli bihaltin,
5   der ruchi uns di gnadi zi gebin,
daz wir immir insamint imo lebin,
daz wir schinin in simo hovi
mid vil michilimo lobi,
daz wir in muzzin gesehin
10   in der himilischin Hiersalem.

If war was engaged anywhere
it was stilled completely by his power
as God himself ordained.
10   *Rex pacificus* ruled then.

24   Solomon was magnificent.
His wealth was beyond measure.
May he who rules in heaven
and should sustain his people
5   deign to grant us his favor
so that we might live with him forever,
so that we might shine in his court
with very great praise,
so that we might behold him
10   in the heavenly Jerusalem.

HISTORIA JUDITH

DIE DREI JÜNGLINGE IM FEUEROFEN

1 E got giborin wurdi,
  do wilt er aller dirri werldi.
  daz lut was heidin
  undi was doch undirscheidin.
 5 dar undir warin,
  di dir von goti larin:
  daz warin di herrin,
  di gutin Israhelin.
  ein andir si sagitin,
 10 also si gilesin habitin,
  daz got wæri uffi demo himili
  sam giwaltig sami hi nidini.

2 Ein kunic hiz Nabuchodonosor.
  den richin got den virkos er,
  sinu abgot er worchti
  ani gotis vorchti,
 5 eni sul guldin
  widir demo himilischin kunigi.
  do sprach uzzir der suli
  daz dicki was ungihuiri:
  si wantin, daz iz wari
 10 der ir heilæri,
  si irvultin alli sin gibot,
  si giloubtin vil vasti an du abgot.

3 Do luitin simo zisamini
  mid trumbin joch mid cymbilin,
  mid phigilin undi swegilbeinin,
  mid rottin undi mid lyrin,
 5 mid phiffin undi mid sambuce:
  so lobitin si den grimmin.

THE STORY OF JUDITH

THE THREE YOUTHS IN THE FURNACE

1   Before God was born
          he ruled over all the world.
          The people were heathen,
          yet they were not all the same.
5   Among them there were those
          who had read about God.
          They were the ones who were pre-eminent,
          the worthy Israelites.
          They told each other
10   what they had read:
          that God is as powerful
          in heaven as here below.

2   There was a king called Nebuchadnezzar.
          He disdained almighty God.
          Not fearing God,
          he had fashioned his idols:
5   a golden pillar
          in opposition to the heavenly king.
          Then, out of the pillar,
          things were spoken that were often monstrous.
          They thought
10   it was their savior.
          They obeyed all his commandments.
          They believed unshakeably in the idols.

3   In concert they played
          trombones and cymbals,
          fiddles and bone pipes,
          rotes and lyres,
5   pipes and sambucas.
          Thus they praised the dreadful one.

mid so gitanimo giluti
so bigingin si sini ziti.

4   Dar komin dri herrin,
di dir goti lib warin.
der eini hiz Sydrac,
dir andir Misac,
5   dir dritti Abdenago.
voni goti bridigotin sin do.
den heidin kunic woltin si bicherin,
er niwolti si niwicht horin.

5   Der kuninc hiz do wirchin
einin ovin erinin.
den hizzer dri dagi eddin,
du dru kint zi demo ovini leiddin:
5   ob min in daz fur nanti,
daz si ir got irchantin;
ob si daz fuir sahin,
daz si sinin got jahin.
du dru kint sprachin vor demi vuri:
10   'dinu abgot sint ungihuiri;
wir giloubin ani den Crist,
der gischuf alliz daz dir ist,
der dir hiz werdin
den himil joch di erdin;
15   sin ist al der ertrinc.
kunic Nabochodonosor, dinu abgot sint ein drugidinc!'

6   Der kunic hiz di heidini gen zisamini,
dragin du dru kint zi dem ovini.
wi ubili sis ginuzzin,
di sin den ovin schuzzin!
5   daz fuir slug in ingegini,
iz virbranti der heidinin eini michil menigi.
got mid sinir giwalt
machit in den ovini kalt.
di uzzirin brunnin,
10   di innirin sungin:

They celebrated his hours
with music of this sort.

4   Three highborn men came there
        who were beloved of God.
        One was called Shadrac,
        the other Mishac,
5   the third Abednego.
        They preached to them about God.
        They wanted to convert the heathen king.
        He refused to hear a thing they had to say.

5   Then the king had an oven
        made of brass.
        He had it heated for three days
        and had the three youths led to the oven.
5   If they were told about the fire,
        they would remain certain of their god.
        If they saw the fire,
        they would affirm his god.
        In front of the fire the three youths said:
10   "Your idols are monsters.
        We believe in Christ,
        who created all that there is,
        whose word brought
        heaven and earth into existence.
15   The entire world is his.
        King Nebuchadnezzar, your idols are phantoms."

6   The king called the heathen together
        and had them carry the three youths to the oven.
        How those who hurled them into the oven
        had to pay for it!
5   The fire lashed out at them.
        It burned up a large number of heathen.
        God in his might
        made the oven cold for the youths.
        Those outside burned.
10   Those inside sang.

do sungin si dar inni
du suzzirin stimmi,
do sungin sin dem ovini
'gloria tibi, domine!
15   deus meus, laudamus te.'
si lobitin Crist in dem ovini.

7   Also di heidini daz gisahin,
vil harti si zwivilotin.
also harti so si gitorstin,
so lobitin si den vurstin.
5   si sprachin, daz unsir got wæri
ein vil gut helphæri,
daz er mid sinir giwalt
machit in den ovin calt
undi er mid simo drosti
10   du dru kint also sampfti irlosti.
Der kunic Nabuchodonosor undi sinu abgot
wurdin beidu zi Babylonia gilastirot.

Die ältere Judith

8   Ein herzogi hiz Holoferni,
der streit widir goti gerni.
er hiz di alliri wirsistin man
sinin siti lernin,
5   daz si warin nidic
undi niminni gnadich,
noch uzzir iri mundi
niman nicheini guoti redi vundi,
niheini guoti antwurti
10   wan mid iri scarphin swerti.

9   'Wazzir undi vuri
mach in vili duiri,
undi sich swer dir ebreschin icht kan,
daz iri nibilibi lebindic niman.'

Those within the oven sang
with sweeter voices
when they sang
"Gloria tibi, domine!

15 Deus meus, laudamus te."
They praised Christ in the oven.

7   When the heathen saw this,
their faith was shaken to its core.
They praised the prince of heaven
as much as they dared.

5   They declared that our God is
a most excellent helper,
that he, through his power,
had made the oven cold for the youths,
and that he, through his solicitude,

10   had saved the three youths with great ease.
Both King Nebuchadnezzar and his idols
were denounced in Babylon.

THE EARLIER STORY OF JUDITH

8   There was a general named Holofernes
who took pleasure in fighting against God.
He had the very worst men
learn his ways,

5   so that they were full of malice
and showed no mercy to anyone,
nor did anyone ever
hear a good word from their mouths,
nor any fitting response —

10   except with their sharp swords.

9   "Make water and fire
scarce among them,
and see that not a single person
remains alive who knows any Hebrew."

5   daz was dir argisti lib.
      sit slug in Judith ein wib.

10   Oloferni do giwan
      ein heri michil undi vreissam
      an der selbin stunt,
      der heidin manic tuisint.
5   er reit verri hini westir
      durch du gotis lastir;
      da bisazzir eini burch, du hezzit Bathania:
      da slug in du schoni Juditha.

11   Do sazzer drumbi, daz is war,
      mer danni ein jar,
      daz er mid sinin gnechtin
      alli dagi gi zi deri burc vechtin.
5   di drinni warin,
      des hungiris nach irchomin;
      di dir vori sazzin,
      di spisi gari gazzin.

12   Do sprach Oloferni
      (di burc habit er gerni):
      'nu hat mich michil wundir,
      daz habit ich gerni irvundin,
5   an wen disi burgæri jehin
      odir ani wen si sich helphi virsehin
      odir wer in helphi dingi;
      si sint nach an dem endi.'

13   Do sprach der burcgravi:
      'swigint, Oloferni!
      wir giloubin an den Crist,
      der dir gischuf alliz daz dir ist,
5   der dir hiz werdin
      den himil joch di erdin;
      sin ist al der ertrinc!
      kuninc Nabuchodonosor, dinu abgot sint ein drugidinc!'

5 He was the wickedest person alive.
 Later he was killed by a woman, Judith.

10 Then and there
 Holofernes assembled
 a huge and destructive army
 of many thousand heathen.
5 He rode far into the west
 in order to defile God.
 There he besieged a city called Bethany.
 There he was killed by the beautiful Judith.

11 In truth, he laid siege there
 more than a year,
 so that he and his soldiers
 might attack the city every day.
5 Those who were inside
 nearly perished from hunger.
 Those who camped in front
 ate all the food.

12 Holofernes spoke.
 He wanted to possess the city.
 "I am quite amazed.
 I would like to find out
5 whom the inhabitants of this city claim as their lord
 or from whom they are hoping for help
 or who might promise them help.
 Their end is near."

13 The burgrave replied:
 "Be still, Holofernes!
 We believe in Christ,
 who created all that there is,
5 whose word brought
 heaven and earth into existence.
 The entire world is his.
 King Nebuchadnezzar, your idols are phantoms!"

14   Do sprach abir einir
      der selbin burgæri:
      'nu giwin uns eini vrist, biscof Bebilin:
      ob iz uwiri gnadi megin sin,
  5   ir giwinnit uns eini vrist,
      so lanc so undir drin tagin ist,
      ob unsich got durch sini guti
      losi uzzi dirri noti.
      nilos er unsich nicht danni,
 10   in dirri burc dingi swer so dir welli!'

15   Do gided du guti Judith
      (du zi goti wol digiti),
      su hizzir machin ein bat,
      ze wari sag ich u daz:
  5   su was diz allir schonis wib,
      su zirti woli den ir lib.
      su undi ir wib Ava,
      di gingin zi wari
      uzzir der burgi
 10   undir di heidinischi menigi.

16   Do sprach Oloferni
      (di burc habit er gerni):
      'nu dar, kamirari,
      ir machit mirz bigahin!
  5   ich gisihi ein wib lussam
      dort ingegin mir gan;
      mir niwerdi daz schoni wib,
      ich virlusi den lib:
      daz ich giniti minis libis
 10   insamint demo sconin wibi!'

17   Di kamirari daz gihortin,
      wi schiri si dar kertin!
      di vrowin si uf hubin,
      in daz gezelt si si drugin.
  5   do sprach du guti Judith
      (du zi goti woli digiti):

14 Next one of the inhabitants
of the city spoke:
"Gain some time for us now, Bishop Bebelin.
If you would be so gracious,

5 obtain a break for us
that lasts three days
so that we can see if God in his goodness
will save us from this peril.
If he does not save us,

10 then let whoever wants dispose of things in this city!"

15 Then the excellent Judith began to act —
she who prayed fervently to God.
She had a bath prepared for herself.
I tell you truly,

5 she was the most beautiful woman of all.
She adorned herself exquisitely.
She and her maidservant Ava,
it is true, went
out of the city

10 among the heathen multitude.

16 Then Holofernes spoke.
He wanted to possess the city.
"Get moving, chamberlains.
Hurry up and do this for me.

5 I see a lovely woman there
coming towards me.
If that beautiful woman does not become mine
I will perish.
Let me enjoy myself

10 together with that beautiful woman!"

17 The chamberlains heard what he said.
How quickly they went to her!
They picked up the woman.
They carried her into the tent.

5 Then the most excellent Judith spoke —
she who prayed fervently to God.

         'nu daz also wesin sol,
         daz du, kuninc, mich zi wibi nemin solt,
         wirt du brutlouft gitan,
10   iz vreiskin wib undi man.
         nu heiz dragin zisamini
         di spisi also manigi!'
         do sprach Oloferni:
         'vrowi, daz dun ich gerni.'

18   Do hiz min dragin zisamini
         di spisi also manigi,
         mit alli di spisi du in demo heri was,
         zi wari sagin ich u daz.
  5   do schancti du guoti Judith
         (du zi goti woli digiti),
         su undi iri wib Ava,
         di schanctin wol zi wari.
         der zenti saz uffin der banc,
10   der hetti din win an dir hant.
         do dranc Holoferni
         (di burc di habit er gerni):
         durch des wibis vruti
         er wart des winis mudi.

19   Den kunic druc min slaffin;
         Judith du stal im daz waffin.
         do gi su vallin an diz gras,
         su betti als ir was.
  5   su sprah 'nu hilf mir, alwaltintir got,
         der mir zi lebini gibot,
         daz ih disi armin giloubigin
         irlosi von den heidinin.'

20   Do irbarmot iz doch
         den alwantintin got.
         do santer ein eingil voni himili,
         der kuntiz deri vrowin hi nidini:
  5   'nu stant uf, du guoti Judith
         (du zi goti woli digiti),

"My king, now
that you are going to make me your wife,
if you organize a marriage festival
10   everyone will find out.
Have as much food
brought in as possible!"
Holofernes replied:
"Lady, I am happy to do so."

18   Then they had all sorts of food
carried in,
all the food, I tell you truly,
that was in the army.
5   The excellent Judith served the wine —
she who prayed fervently to God.
She and her maidservant Ava
served the wine very expertly indeed.
Even the last man on the bench
10   held wine in his hand.
Then Holofernes drank up.
He wanted to possess the city.
Because the woman was clever
the wine made him tired.

19   The king was carried to sleep.
Judith stole his weapon from him.
Then she went out and fell prostrate on the grass.
She prayed as her feelings moved her.
5   She said: "Almighty God, who ordained that I be born,
now help me
to rescue the unfortunate faithful
from these heathen."

20   Then almighty God
took pity.
He sent an angel from heaven.
He revealed to the woman down below what she was to do.
5   "Now stand up, most excellent Judith —
she who prayed fervently to God —

unde geinc dir zi demo gizelti,
da daz swert si giborgin.
du heiz din wib Avin
10   vur daz betti gahin,
ob er uf welli,
daz su in eddewaz dwelli.
du zuh iz wiglichi
undi sla vravillichi,
15   du sla Holoferni
daz houbit von dem buchi.
du la ligin den satin buch,
daz houbit stoz in ginin stuchin
undi genc widir
20   in zi der burgi.
dir gibutit got voni himili,
daz du irlosis di israhelischin menigi.'

and go into the tent
where the sword is hidden.
Tell your maidservant Ava
10   to go quickly and stand in front of the bed
so that, if he wants to get up,
she can delay him somewhat.
You will draw the sword as if in battle
and thrust boldly.
15   You will cut Holofernes's
head from his trunk.
You will leave the sated trunk lying there.
Stick the head in your long sleeve
and go back
20   into the city.
God in heaven commands you
to save the people of Israel."

Notes

Earlier Ezzolied

2.1   "The light in the darkness" (John 1.5).

2.5   "In the beginning was the word" (John 1.1).

3.5   It seems likely that the later version of the *Ezzolied* retains the
        correct reading of this line: "[Lord] of earth and of heaven" (6.5).
        This makes better sense of the "four" elements mentioned a few
        lines below.

4.4–5   These lines translate Genesis 1.26, *Faciemus hominem ad imag-
        inem et similitudinem nostram*, "Let us make man in our image and
        likeness."

Later Ezzolied

1.10   The line has provoked much discussion, since it is hard to imagine
        that *everyone* who heard the song would have become a monk.
        Some have suggested that the song was composed to celebrate the
        reformation of the Bamberg canons, each of whom then hastened
        to become a *better* monk. But why would a *German* song have been
        composed for such an occasion? Others, referring to the statement
        in the *Vita Altmanni* that the song was written on a pilgrimage (see
        introduction), have suggested the line means that everyone, on
        hearing the song, put on the garb of a pilgrim — which is similar to
        that of a monk.

12.5–6 This recalls Matthew 11.9, *plus quam prophetam*, "more than a
        prophet."

12.9–12 These lines combine Matthew 3.3, *Vox clamantis in deserto:
        Parate viam Domini: rectas facite semitas eius,* "A voice crying in

the wilderness: Prepare a way for the lord, make straight his paths," with Luke 1.17, *et ipse praecedet ante illum in spiritu et virtute Eliae*, "And he will precede him in the spirt and in the power of Elijah."

13.3   The division of history into six ages, after the six days of Creation, goes back to Augustine. Ordinarily Christ's birth marks the beginning of the sixth age, as it does in *Annolied* 4.3. Ezzo follows another tradition, according to which the six days correspond to six ages, each of which lasts a thousand years (after Psalm 89.4). Since the six thousand years of history can also be understood as a single day in which the lord will come in the eleventh hour (after Matthew 20.1–16), then Christ must be born in the year 5500, half way through the sixth age.

13.9   "At the end of time."

15.8   "Glory in the highest" (Luke 2.14).

17.1   "Ancient of days" (Daniel 7.9, 13, 22), said of God.

21.9–10   See introduction, p. 9.

22.1   Jesus is called high priest in Hebrews 3.1, 6.20.

23.1–2   The part is his soul, which was separated from his body when he descended into hell.

24.1–2, 5   These lines cite Isaiah 63.1, *Quis est iste, qui venit de Edom, tinctis vestibus de Bosra? Iste formosus in stola sua*, "Who is this coming from Edom, coming from Bozrah, his garments stained red? Beautiful in his clothes. . . ."

25.7   "He who is strongly armed" (Luke 11.21), interpreted as referring to the Devil.

25.11   Draws on Mark 3.27.

26.1–10   The sacrifice brought by Abel prefigures the sacrifice on the cross. Abraham's sacrifice of Isaac (Genesis 22.1–13) prefigures God's sacrifice of his son. According to John 3.14, Moses lifting up the snake prefigures Christ.

27   The blood of the Passover lamb prefigures the blood of Christ, which offers freedom and salvation.

28.8   "on the altar of the cross."

30.1   "Spiritual Israel."

30.4   "from Pharaoh's yoke."

31.1   "O blessed cross."

32.3–6   *Et ego si exaltatus fuero a terra, omnia traham ad me ipsum* (John 12.32), "And if I am lifted up from the earth I will draw all men to myself."

33.1   "O cross of the saviour."

33.1–12   Life as a ship journey has a long tradition, going back to antiquity. Christians developed the idea into a complex allegory.

ANNOLIED

2.2   These lines cite John 1.1, "voice" taking the place of the "word." "Light" is drawn from John 1.4–5.

2.10   This idea is derived from the somewhat heterodox teaching concerning the Creation formulated by John Scotus Eriugena (9th century), according to whom humankind, the "third world," combines the two other "worlds" of spirit and matter.

2.15   According to Greek philosophers and Greek Church Fathers, humans (the microcosm) contain within themselves all of creation (the macrocosm).

4.3   See note to *Ezzolied*, 13.3.

5.2   The sending out of the apostles is based on Matthew 28.19; the site of their missionary work derives partly from Acts, partly from legendary traditions.

6.1   On the mythical origin of the Franks see the note to 22.3.

8.5   Ninus was considered the founder of the Assyrian empire and the builder of Nineveh. First mentioned in the *Persika* of Ctesias, he appears later in the works of Augustine and the third-century historian Justinus.

9.10   The dimensions of Nineveh are probably taken from Jonah 3.3–4.

11.1   According to the vision in Daniel 7, four animals come out of the sea: a lion with wings of an eagle, a bear with three very large teeth, a winged leopard, and a beast with iron teeth that has ten horns, three of which are displaced by a small horn. These animals were interpreted as representing the empires of the Medes, Persians, Greeks, and Selucids, whose destruction would bring the liberation of the Jews. The scheme was later revised to accommodate the Romans, so that the order of empires, as in the *Annolied*, is Babylonians, Medes and Persians, Macedonians, and Romans.

16   According to Jerome, who decided the fourth animal was a boar, the ten horns represent ten kings who will split up the Roman empire. The writer of the *Annolied* revises the elements in ways that are more favorable for Rome: the iron claws and teeth represent power and freedom; the ten horns are now ten allies.

18.12   This must refer to Caesar's wars against the Gauls — which the patriotic author of the *Annolied* has transposed to Germany.

19.7   Isidore of Seville makes a connection between a Mons Suevo and the Swabians (*Etymologies,* 9.2.98).

20.9   *Noricus ensis* is from Horace, *Odes*, 1.16.9 and *Epodes* 17.71.

20.15–16   This is the earliest reference to the Armenian origins of the Bavarians. It is also mentioned in the *Vita Altmanni* (see introduction).

20.16   In classical times Armenia was part of the Persian empire, which enables the *Annolied* to establish a connection between the Bavarians (20) and the Persians (13).

21.23   The etymological relation advanced here between *sahs* and *Sachsen*, "Saxon," is probably accurate.

22.3   The Trojan origin of the Franks was common knowledge in the Middle Ages. The *Annolied* is the second text that attempts to ground the continuity of the Empire in the genealogical connection between Romans and Franks.

23.20   Xanten (from Ad Santos) was known in the second century as Colonia Trajana (after the emperor Trajan) and soon after as Colonia Trojana (after the Trojans). In the eleventh century it was sometimes called Troy.

25.1   Ancient sources provide no support for the role ascribed to the Germans in these strophes. In the *Pharsalia*, on which the writer of the *Annolied* draws for this passage, Lucan refers to a rumor that the tribes between the Rhine and the Elbe followed Caesar. But he dismisses it as false (1.481–83). The second-century historian Florus reports that the battle of Pharsalus was decided by Caesar's Gallic and Germanic allies.

25.4   From the end of the tenth century *Gallia* was used to refer to the German regions west, *Germania* to those east of the Rhine. According to the *Kaiserchronik* (395–99), Trier is in *Gallia*.

28.7   This is the earliest appearance of this explanation for the use of the plural pronoun as a sign of respect. Subsequently it was cited often.

29.11   Actually, Cologne was named after Agrippina, daughter of Germanicus and wife of the emperor Claudius. After the city became a *colonia* in A.D. 50, its name became Colonia Agrippinensis.

30.13   Ordinarily the kings were crowned in Aachen. However, in 1077 a rival king was crowned in Mainz, and in 1106 Henry VI was crowned there. These facts provide one of the few clues to the dating of the poem.

32.25   The fourth-century bishop Maternus is the first recorded bishop of Cologne. The earliest record of the legend that is told here dates from the ninth century, a time when many bishoprics were trying to trace their history back to the age of the apostles.

34.6   This probably refers to the emperor's decision to support Anno's candidacy as archbishop of Cologne in spring 1056.

39.1–2   This may refer to Anno's struggles with Landgraf Heinrich of Lorraine, who had to relinquish Siegburg to Anno and who died, insane, in 1061.

39.8   The revolt of the citizens of Cologne against Anno in 1074.

40.1–4   The Saxon Wars of 1073–75, which have been expanded to cover the entire Holy Roman Empire.

42.11–12   Bardo was bishop of Mainz, 1031–51. Heribert was bishop of Cologne, 999–1021. Arnold (or Arnulf), who figures in the next section, was bishop of Worms, 1044–65.

43.23   According to one account, Anno called back those he had driven out of Cologne — said to be more than six hundred merchants, whose departure had left the city desolate. At Easter 1075 he received them back into the church and returned their possessions.

49.15–16   The Bible mentions only one sister of Moses, Miriam, who is stricken with leprosy and then cured miraculously (Numbers 12).

Kaiserchronik

247   *Kaiserchronik* vv. 270–62 is taken, sometimes with substantial changes, from the following parts of the *Annolied* and Priester Arnolt's *Von der Siebenzahl*:

270–378   corresponds to *Annolied* 19.1–23.26
455–525   corresponds to *Annolied* 24.1–28.12
526–90   corresponds to *Annolied* 11.1–17.14
591–96   corresponds to *Annolied* 28.13–18
603–04   corresponds to *Annolied* 29.1–2
605–42   corresponds to *Von der Siebenzahl* 640–95
643–49   corresponds to *Annolied* 29.7–14
651–60   corresponds to *Annolied* 30.15–24
661–62   corresponds to *Annolied* 29.3–4.

300–301   This is the earliest mention of Boimunt and Ingram, who do not appear in the *Annolied*.

392–94   May refer to the murder of archbishop Adalbert, 1160.

399   See note to *Annolied* 25.4.

404   Labienus (Labian), Caesar's principal subordinate in Gaul, conducted military operations in 54–53 BCE against the Treveri and their leader Indutiomarus (Dulzmar). After the Roman victory, Cingetorix, Indutiomarus's son-in-law who had earlier sided with the Romans, was installed as a client king. Vercingetorix (Signator) led an unsuccessful revolt against the Romans in which the Treveri did not take part. The rather different relations of these figures in the *Kaiserchronik* derive from the *Gesta Treverorum*.

Lob Salomons

1.1   "Illustrious light of the world." The line refers to John 8.12, *Ego sum lux mundi*, "I am the light of the world."

6.5   Some have suggested this must be the lost *Archaiologia* of the Phoenicians by Hieronymus Aegyptus that is mentioned in Josephus Flavius. However, the text says only that Jerome *found* this marvel in a Greek *Archaiologia*. There is evidence of such a work, falsely attributed to Eusebius, but now lost, that contained material about Solomon. St. Jerome, who translated Eusebius's *Chronicon*, is here credited with discovering material in the lost *Archaiologia*, another work (thought to be) by Eusebius.

10.7 "light and brightness."

10.8 "sweetness."

12.4 "incense and wealth."

13.2 The ambiguous *ferculum* of Song of Songs 3.9 was often taken to mean table. Honorious Augustodunensis interpreted it anagogically to mean Holy Scripture, the four legs representing the four levels of literal and allegorical meaning that are to be found in Scripture. In this spirit, the last two lines of the strophe invite the allegorical reading that is then offered in strophes 20–22.

14.7 "steps."

17.8 "military might."

21.1–2 That the queen is here taken to represent the Church (*ecclesia*) and is married to Christ, means she is not only the queen of Sheba, but also the bride in the Song of Songs, which was read in the Middle Ages as an allegory of the marriage of Christ and his Church.

21.6 "united with God in communion."

22.9 *Tibi sacrificabo hostiam laudis* (Psalms 115.17), "I will bring you an offering of praise."

23.10 "king of peace."

HISTORIA JUDITH

6.14–15 "Glory be to you, Lord! My God, we praise you."

13.3–8 These lines repeat 5.11–16. See introduction, p. 6.